THE RUNNERS' REPAIR MANUAL

THE RUNNERS' REPAIR MANUAL

A Complete Program for Diagnosing and Treating Your Foot, Leg and Back Problems

by Dr. Murray F. Weisenfeld with Barbara Burr

St. Martin's Press, New York

To my wife Shirley who makes the sun shine.
To those runners who share their agonies and
ecstasies with me.
To Dr. and Mrs. R. O. Schuster who made it possible.

Copyright © 1980 by Murray F. Weisenfeld and Barbara Burr.

All rights reserved. For information, write:
St. Martin's Press, Inc., 175 Fifth Ave., New York, N.Y. 10010.
Manufactured in the United States of America

Exercise illustrations by Lori Weisenfeld
Technical illustrations by Gary Tong

Design: Paul Chevannes

Library of Congress Cataloging in Publication Data

Weisenfeld, Murray F
    The runners' repair manual.

    1. Foot—Wounds and injuries. 2. Running—Accidents and injuries.
I. Burr, Barbara, joint author. II. Title.
RD563.W43   617'.585'044   79-26794
ISBN 0-312-69596-9

Acknowledgments

We want to thank all the runners and doctors and other people who helped us write this book.

Thanks to the doctors who contributed so much—Dr. Stanley Roman, osteopath; Dr. Seymour (Mac) Goldstein, chiropractor; Dr. Richard Schuster and Dr. Dennis Richard, podiatrists; Dr. Louis Galli and Dr. Josef Geldwert, podiatrists; and Dr. Ed Colt, endocrinologist. And a special thanks to Dr. George Sheehan, who has done so much for sports medicine. He also sent my co-author to me when she had an injury—and that's how this book got started.

Thanks to Melissa Hayden for her expert help on exercises and body-training.

Thanks to Mitch Maslin for his advice on shoes, and to Bob Glover, an expert on training runners, among other things.

Thanks to our invaluable secretary, Lyn Palter.

Thanks to marathon coordinator Allan Steinfeld, who gave us valuable statistics and insights on the New York City Marathon.

Thanks to my patients who gave their time and knowledge to the book—Dick Traum, Molly Colgan, Jane Killion, Barbara Backer, Nancy Tighe, and Kathy and Bill Horton.

A special thanks to my patients/friends who posed for the cover picture—Michael Cleary, Fritz Mueller, Fred Lebow, Jane Killion, Laurie McBride, and George Klas.

Contents

Foreword About the Evolution of the Foot

The evolution of man's foot is a history of constant change in function and form. The foot as we know it is a relative newcomer in terms of evolutionary time—and that's usually the problem.

Man's foot was not originally designed for walking, much less running long distances. The modern foot evolved out of the fin of some primordial fish and these fins pointed backward. Contrary to what most believe, fins are used more for stability in the water than for locomotion. Locomotion was a function of the tail and is still partly a function of the lower spine in most creatures, including man.

These fins ultimately evolved into fin-feet of amphibians. They pointed more sideways and functioned like oars of a boat in water—and on land—and were not considered maximally efficient movers in either environment.

The reptile that evolved out of the amphibian developed the first recognizable "ankle," "knee" and "hip" joints. It was capable of lifting the body off the ground and while the leg still pointed more sideways than forward, the feet had the capability of rotating in the forward direction. Locomotion was primarily the function of the leg but this is the first time feet appear to get into the act of locomotion. In the previous amphibian stage, the feet were little more than base plates for the leg.

Out of the reptile followed the early mammal with feet and legs that pointed almost completely forward. It is the mammalian foot that is most pertinent in this context. Some authorities—especially Dudley Morton of the now famous

Morton's foot—feel that the characteristics of early mammalian feet and many mammalian characteristics for that matter, were intimately associated with the arboreal environment—trees and underbrush. The structure of these early mammalian feet certainly suggests some form of tree adaptation. These were probably rather generalized feet adapting somewhat to both ground and "branch" surfaces but probably not well adapted to either.

Apparently at this time in mammalian evolution something less than a hundred million years ago, some group of early mammals "chose" the tree environment for permanent habitation. They adapted to the tree environment for tens of millions of years and gave rise to all manner of monkeys and apes, including man's ancestors. During this very considerable evolutionary time span, the foot of man's ancestors became highly adapted to the tree environment.

Before mentioning the influence of the tree environment on the human foot, we cannot completely dismiss those other mammals who chose not to evolve in the trees, but adapted to the ground instead. While they are not in man's lineage, they have in general a much longer history of foot adaptation to the ground and are more completely adapted to the ground than the feet of man. Not that any of us would want to run around on paws or hooves, but an awareness of this kind of development and how they got there is often helpful to doctors in treating people with foot problems, particularly running foot problems.

Concerning the influence of the tree in the evolution of the human foot: We can imagine that if we were to climb or live in trees, it would be much easier if we had a pair of strong hands where we now have feet. While very few of us have reason to think this way, this is just what nature provided our ancestors with during those tens of millions of years of tree habitation. Anthropologists actually describe our primate ancestors as being "fourhanded."

The grasping foot was absolutely essential for survival in the trees. This is another way of saying that it was also one of the elements for development in the manlike direction. The grasping foot permitted the creature to squat on branches without falling out. With this secure perch, it could begin to reach out for food. Here we see the importance of grasping feet in developing different capabilities in the fore limbs and rear limbs. Reaching led to standing and holding. This, in turn, led to the first bipedal steps on the tops of branches. There is no question that with grasping hands and feet that man's ancestors could walk four-legged quite easily on the tops of branches. However, the ability to walk on two feet had a survival advantage in liberating the arms for other uses. We are inclined to think that those primitive two-legged "first steps" might have been running steps, since it is easier to maintain balance with a bit of speed.

The freeing of the hands and the ability to reach made way for an additional mode of locomotion—swinging (brachiation). Hanging and swinging under a branch tended to straighten the basically four-legged body and was a preadaptation for development in the erect bipedal direction that followed.

It seems like a paradox that the highly specialized foot characteristics that were so essential for survival in the trees and for the continued evolution of man's ancestors were rather incompatible for the use to which they would someday be put. For example, the foot was structured for a generally round surface and for this the foot had to be extremely flexible. The four outer toes were used as "wrap around" hooks and tended to be long. The first toe (the big toe) served as "back up" for the grasp. It was not all that necessary so it remained short.

The roundness of branches induced curves, slants and twists into the foot segments. This can be visualized if the relaxed hand is placed palm down on a table. Note the slant of the four outer knuckles and the low position of the first knuckle. Notice how the fingers are curved and the fingers and fingernails seem to lay a bit on the side—and how the first finger and its nail lay in the opposite direction.

And traces of tree-adapting characteristics, as seen in the

hand for example, must be discarded before a foot can function well on the ground. Unfortunately, nature is slow to adapt structures to new function.

Authorities do not agree as to when man's ancestors came out of the trees. Estimates range from twelve million years ago to twenty-five million years ago or even more. No matter. The only thing that is reasonably certain is that there has not been enough time (plus a few other factors) to eliminate all traces of tree adaptation in the human foot. Or, as the anthropologists stated, man's foot is not yet completely adapted to the ground. Only a portion of the population has been endowed with well ground-adapted feet. These people, athletes and non-athletes alike, have less foot problems than most.

Fortunately, foot characteristics that were so useful to our tree-dwelling ancestors and such a problem to modern man, can be recognized as imbalances and properly dealt with, along with the secondary annoyances, the corns, calluses, blisters, et cetera.

Modern living is another factor that contributes to foot problems. The modern individual at work or at leisure is often apt to spend more time on his feet than primitive man. Take for instance the runners who have burst on the scene during the early 70s and show every indication of staying. It is nothing for them to run anywhere from a few miles a week to 150 miles a week, and all this is compounded by hard flat surfaces and sometimes questionable shoes.

But that is what this book is all about.

There are very few doctors who have treated as many athletes, including dancers, as the author of this book—which, in a way, speaks for itself. Besides, he's a fine gentleman.

Richard O. Schuster, D.P.M.

PART ONE

1

"I Tried Running Once and I Didn't Like It"

The Podiatrist's Pain-Free, Injury-Free Way to Start Running

If you haven't started running yet, or you sort-of-started but stopped, then you've got an advantage over a lot of people. Most people don't consult a podiatrist until after they've been running a while—running wrong—and they've got an injury. Now, by reading this book, you're "seeing a podiatrist" before you start—so you can start running right.

I'm not the least bit interested in telling you how to become the fastest runner on your block, or how to increase your mileage as quickly as possible. I just want to save you from the most common mistakes beginners make—mistakes that cause pain and delays in the first few months of running.

In running, an "injury" is not necessarily a twisted kneecap or a broken bone, as it is in other sports. A running injury could be a strained or pulled muscle. It could be a bone in the foot that's bruised from running on hard pavement. It could be a back pain you get because one leg is slightly longer than the other. Weaknesses in your body show up during running. After all, no body's perfect, and running five or six or ten miles can bring out a problem in your feet, legs or back.

But everything in life is a trade-off. You can stay home and keep your feet comfortable. Or you can go out and run and develop a foot problem (which is probably correctable), and also develop firmer muscles, healthier complexion, more energy and stamina and a better disposition.

Bob Glover says many runner's injuries are "diseases of excellence," which I think is very apt.

What I want to do is help prevent the "diseases of ignorance"—injuries you can avoid, if you learn to run properly. You can avoid these unnecessary injuries by following a very simple four-step program that starts you running right.

First of all, I want to correct some wrong ideas you may have. A lot of people don't get started because of all the stuff their running friends tell them. For instance:

- Don't run until you've spent $175 for a stress test.
- Get yourself some $50 running shoes, before you even know if you're going to like the sport.
- Bounce out of bed at 6 A.M. and stretch your body; then go out for a brisk morning run. (Even though your body normally feels about as stretchy as an old log at that hour.)

First, what about a stress test?

In a stress test, your body's responses are measured as you jog on a treadmill or pedal a bike. Many Y's give stress tests, or you can find a local hospital that has a sports medicine division, or a cardiologist who does stress testing.

A stress test is especially recommended if you're very overweight, or have been sedentary, or if you're over forty, or if anything in your medical history indicates heart problems. The American College of Sports Medicine says you should *not* automatically take a stress test; you should ask your doctor if you need one.

But my experience is, most people won't get around to asking their doctors. They keep putting off the visit and they never start running. That's why I feel that if you're moderately out of shape, like most of us before running, you should simply start jogging/walking—the easy-does-it way (which means enjoy yourself). Listen to your body and trust yourself.

I'll give you the basic rules in four lines. Then we'll discuss them a little.

RULE 1: Wear any firm, low-heeled shoes.

RULE 2: Do ten minutes of stretching and strengthening exercises before and after your walk/run session.

RULE 3: Stay in motion fifteen to twenty minutes—jogging or walking.

RULE 4: Do this three times a week—preferably with a day's rest in between each day of running.

Follow these rules and you'll get a good start. After two or three or four weeks, your body will be adjusted to running, and you'll feel like increasing the amount of time you spend running each day. And the number of days you run each week.

At that point, you're ready to buy the right shoes. And this is very important. The right shoes are part of your injury-avoiding strategy, throughout your running career. Chapter 3 will tell you how to select the right shoes for you. And it gives you a checklist to take with you to the shoe store.

Another thing you should do, after your first few weeks, is to read chapter 2 "How to Run Right and Hurt Less." Because, as you start increasing your mileage, where you run and how you run become very important. The wrong running style can cause injuries. Running on the wrong kind of road can cause injuries. But that's not until later, when you're up to a few miles a day.

Right now, let's get back to your beginner's rules and explain them a bit more.

RULE 1: *What to wear*. Dress in layers. For instance, a light sweater with a jacket over it. You heat up when you run, and then you can take off your jacket and tie it around your waist. Wear any firm, low-heeled shoes like sneakers, work shoes, whatever. Of course, running shoes are ideal. But for the first few weeks, you won't be running long distances—so running shoes are not absolutely essential.

RULE 2: *Exercising.* If you don't do your stretching and strengthening exercises, you'll probably get an injury. It's that simple.

Why do you have to stretch? Because running tightens up the muscles in your lower back and the back of your legs. And tight muscles become stiff, tense and painful.

Why do you have to do strengthening exercises? Because running strengthens the back-of-leg muscles much more than it does the front muscles. After you've been running a while, your front leg muscles are relatively weak and prone to injury. Also, your abdominal muscles are weak, compared to your back muscles. So you can get lower-back pains.

The Weisenfeld Workout I give you in the exercise chapter are eight basic exercises I recommend for every runner. This workout is especially important for beginners, because your muscles are more out of shape and more prone to injury. Do the complete workout before you go out to run and do it again when you get back. It takes only a few minutes, and it will protect most beginners from injuries.

A few runners will still get some pains and problems, even if they do this basic workout—because they have a foot imbalance or other physical problem. So I've also given you special exercises for special problems. If you do get a pain, read the section on your injury. It will tell you which exercises to do.

RULE 3: *Jogging/Walking.* The general rule is, just stay in motion for fifteen to twenty minutes—jogging and walking, as your body and feelings direct. For example, you can jog one block, then walk half a block. Jog another block, then walk half a block.

After a week or so, you may feel like running more. You'll want to jog two blocks and walk half a block. Then you'll be jogging four blocks and walking half a block. Eventually, you'll be jogging easily for a full twenty minutes—always at your own pace.

While we're at it, let's talk about pace, or speed of jogging. Always jog at the speed that lets you talk without huffing and puffing. It's good to jog with a friend, so you can talk as you go along. But if one person is a faster runner, you should both jog at the slower person's pace. Or you should jog separately.

I meet so many women who run with their husbands or boyfriends, and the man pushes the woman beyond her natural pace. Don't fall into this trap. It not only ruins the woman's pleasure in the run; it can cause an injury. Not to mention a fight.

The right pace is a "talking" pace. You should be able to talk as easily as if you were sitting at home in a chair. If you start huffing, jog slower or walk. Resume jogging when you can talk without breathing hard. If you're jogging alone, talk aloud to yourself now and then, just to check your breathing.

It's nice to bring your dog along, if you can't find a friend. Then you can talk to your dog. Some people start running with a dog because they're embarrassed to be out running. They think all runners are lean and muscular, so they don't dare appear in running clothes with a potbelly. That's fine. Make it easy for yourself. Just wear your regular jeans or slacks and pretend you're taking your dog for a walk. You'll start to see other less-than-perfect bodies out running. And you'll start to get a good feeling, seeing them. You have a feeling of pride and fellowship with all these other people who are out doing something good for their lives. Just as you are.

RULE 4: *How often to run.* Run three times a week for the first two or three weeks, or longer. Add another running day to your week when you really feel ready for it—not when your ego tells you that you should. It's hard to give a rule for how quickly you should increase your running days. But it's usually better to under-do rather than over-do. I know a lot of people who've "started" running three or four times— because they overdid it and had to rest and start again.

When Do You Stop Being a Beginner?

I'd say when you can jog twenty minutes comfortably and without walking . . . and do this four times a week . . . then you're no longer a beginner.

When are you a runner instead of a jogger? It's up to you. I've heard people specify X minutes per mile for jogging and Y minutes per mile for running. I'll let someone else argue about that. If you feel like you're running, then you're running.

You'll find you pass through your beginner stage naturally, just by increasing the time you spend running, as your body feels ready for it.

Some days, you're so full of energy, you feel like you're flying. The run doesn't seem to take any energy; in fact, it gives you energy, and you're feeling good the rest of the day and looking forward to tomorrow's run. Don't be surprised if tomorrow's run is a downer. You've just hit a small peak, and after a peak, you always go down. Just rest the next day —either skip your run or take it slow and easy. And accept that this is normal. Your body will recover and you'll hit another peak. This is how you make progress.

Serious, advanced runners plan their peaks. They train toward a few big races a year and plan their training so they'll hit a peak on the day of the race. After the peak, their performance is down again for a while. Then they slowly build up to the next peak.

So just keep steadily running and resting, and soon you'll get interested in counting the miles and thinking about entering a race.

At this point, read chapter 2, "How to Run Right and Hurt Less." As I said earlier, the *way* you run and *where* you run can make all the difference in staying injury-free.

In preparing this book, I had a roundtable discussion with several of my patients. And most of them found that their injuries showed up when they started running four or five miles on a fairly regular basis. Here's where you really have to pay attention to your running style. Run with other people

—especially experienced runners—and ask them to correct any errors you're making.

Of course, you may get some injuries, no matter how careful you are and how correctly you run. As I said, no body's perfect, and running for miles a day can put stress on your muscles and structure.

So the best you can do is minimize any injury. As soon as you start feeling pain, run slower. If it doesn't go away, stop running. Go home and consult the "Injuries" section of this book, and learn how to handle the problem before it gets serious.

About the only pain you can safely run through is a side stitch. It helps if you slow down and do some deep diaphragm breathing. This helps relax the stitch. Another remedy is to shout "HA!". I mean really shout. Squeeze the air out of your lungs with a short, forceful yell.

After you've been running a few months, and increasing your mileage, it's fun to start planning for a race. For instance, one runner I know, Kathleen Jordan, started running in January. She set a goal right away—to run the L'Eggs Mini-Marathon in June. That's 6.2 miles. Kathleen is under thirty and in good health, and she did achieve her goal with no problem. She ran the race with her sister-in-law, who had been running for a year and a half but is fifteen years older. The younger woman ran a faster race, but they both had a fine time.

So let your body be your guide, as to when you want to start training for a race. Races are stimulating and sociable and a lot of fun, and I encourage you to do them. But I can't teach you how. There are a lot of books and articles in the runner's magazines that will give you tips on training for races. In this book, I just want to teach you to run properly so you'll stay injury-free.

Don't increase your mileage too soon. Your enthusiasm and your cardiovascular capacity increase faster than your muscular strength and flexibility.

Along about the third day, or the tenth or fourteenth day, you may start feeling uncontrollably good. You're delighted with your health and vigor and a love of exercise that you never knew you had. Suddenly, there's no limit to how much energy you have and how far you can run! Overnight, you've doubled your distance, and you're puffing along at high speed, your face red and your heart pounding.

Next day, your legs are too stiff to walk on when you get out of bed. You're tired, depressed, your muscles are sore and you feel like an idiot for overdoing it—acting like a kid in a candy store.

Well, lots of people make this mistake. But you don't have to. In the long run, you'll get more exercise and you'll advance faster if you increase slowly and gradually.

As I said, your cardiovascular system improves a lot faster than your muscular system. We still don't know exactly what happens, physiologically, when a person overtrains. But we do know that the body protests and you feel rotten and you hold yourself back on the road to better health.

Here's a horrible example of how not to start running.

One of my patients started running in February, 1978. The day before he started, he was a two-pack-a-day smoker and twenty pounds overweight. So he stopped smoking and started running. So far so good. Then he became a born-again runner. He was turned on by the thrill and pleasure of running, of feeling his body change and come alive. He got that glorious desire to run as much as he could. He wasn't working at the time, so he devoted all his time to running, stretching, dieting and resting. He ran from upper Manhattan down to the World Trade Center in the morning and loved every block of it. He ran to the unemployment office. He followed the Marathon Training Program a friend gave him.

Yes, he decided to run the New York City Marathon in October—having just started running in February.

He ran the marathon. That was October, 1978. Nearly a year later, he still wasn't back into running on a steady basis.

Right after the marathon, he got the "I don't wanna run"

blues that so many overstressed runners get. That lasted a few months. He ran some more and got a groin pull. His feet and legs kept bothering him. He still considers himself a runner and will probably get back to it. But look at all the months he's lost. Look at the price he's paid, just to run those glorious 26.2 miles of the marathon. He would have run more if he'd gone slower.

You probably won't overdo to this extent.

But many people do the same thing on a smaller scale. They run too far before they're ready, and then they get aches, pains and injuries and they slow down their running progress.

So be smart. Let your progress come naturally. Don't push it. As they say, don't push the river, it flows by itself. And you grow by yourself. Have you ever seen a flower pushing itself to grow faster?

It isn't necessary.

You'll probably hear the general rule that it's safe to increase your mileage 10 percent a week. This is okay as a general rule. But you may find it's too much for you, some weeks. If you're under pressure on the job, and you start putting pressure on your running—pushing yourself to increase your distance each week—you'll probably catch a cold or pull a muscle or start getting some of the other symptoms of overstress—like aching legs, lack of interest in running, irritability, tiredness without being able to sleep.

Please, be smart. Learn your own body language and listen to it, throughout your running career.

If you have tried running before, and didn't like it, it's probably because you followed the good old American way of exercise which is "go out and kill yourself." It's no good unless it hurts.

I'm not an expert on Eastern and Western philosophies, but I have taken some yoga. And I was very impressed by one thing they taught us. They told us to take the position we were practicing and stretch to the degree that was comfortable for us. Then hold it in that comfortable position.

Did you ever hear anything so revolutionary? Be *comfortable*? In an exercise class? Don't push yourself, don't hurt yourself, let your body be your guide? I was shocked. And so relieved.

And then I realized a commonsense thing: if you enjoy your exercise today, you'll exercise again tomorrow. If you hate your exercise because you're pushing yourself, you'll eventually find a reason to stop the exercise—whether it's running or pushups or anything else.

I also discovered, in my yoga class, that if you stretch to the limit of your comfort, your comfort-limit stretches. A few classes later, you feel comfortable stretching farther.

Running is like that.

If you jog as much as is comfortable for two weeks, then at the end of two weeks your comfortable jogging-range will naturally be greater. Those yogis learned a thing or two about the human body, over the centuries. A lot more than the drill sergeant in the gym class you took as a kid or as an adult.

How do you learn to trust yourself? By listening to your body. If you're like most of us, your body has to go to extraordinary extremes to get your attention—like giving you a cold or an ulcer or a pulled muscle. Use running as an opportunity to start getting smart. Start listening to the quieter clues your body is giving you—like irritable fatigue (as opposed to pleasant fatigue)—sleeplessness—hard, brutal soreness, as opposed to pleasant soreness.

This "trust yourself" technique is the secret of remaining injury-free as you go on in running. The runner who pushes himself beyond his limit is the one who gets injuries. Say you've advanced to the point where you're comfortably running five or six miles a day. One week, you start feeling your oats and you push it up to ten miles a day, on a regular basis. That's when I'll expect to see you in my office with runner's knee or Achilles tendonitis or any one of the injuries runners afflict themselves with.

So get out, get started and enjoy. Just remember the slogan of smart runners: Easy does it. But do it.

2
How to Run right and Hurt Less

Advice for Beginning and
Experienced Runners

Do you really have to learn how to run?

You ran when you were two- or three-years old and never
stopped running till you were about twelve, if you're a woman,
or sometime later, if you're a man.

So why don't you just go out and run now? Do you really
need a podiatrist to tell you how?

Judging by all the pulls and pains and injuries I see—
injuries caused by the wrong running habits—I'd say you
probably do. It's worth your while to take a few minutes to
learn the right way to run.

There are two differences between your childhood running
and the running you do today. First, you're older. Your body
doesn't have the flexibility you had as a kid—so it doesn't
recover as quickly from any damage you inflict on it.

Your body *will* become stronger and more flexible as you
run and exercise properly. Your muscles will be more resilient.
Some of your bones will probably become thicker. Your lungs
will be stronger. Your heart will be more efficient. But you've

got to run properly—or your running can hurt you instead of strengthening you.

The second difference is that as a kid you never ran the long distances you're doing now. Kids run in short spurts, then stop to hit a ball or climb a tree. Today, people run one to ten miles a day—and each foot hits the ground about 800 times in every mile. So if you're making a wrong move, you're doing it hundreds and thousands of times—until you get swollen tendons, inflamed knees, aching heels, bruised bones and a sore back.

Podiatrists see more people with running injuries than any other kind of doctor. Every day we see what the wrong running habits can do to you. And we've come to know what's the best way to run, to avoid injuries.

So learn the few simple principles involved in running right. And you'll run with more energy and less strain. Every run will benefit your body instead of hurting it.

Keep Your Spine in Line

The right way to run is to stand straight up with your weight directly over your hips. Don't lean forward. When you lean forward, you're pulling harder on the calf muscles. This can be one of the causes of Achilles tendonitis, shin splints or just sore calf muscles.

You see a lot of young runners leaning forward. They probably think it gets them there faster, or at least makes them look faster. Don't do it. Your spine should be straight, your shoulders should be low and relaxed, not hunched up.

You have to watch out for the tendency to lean forward—especially when you're tired. Sometimes you even feel like you're falling forward. This is understandable, since running and walking are done by falling forward and then putting your foot out to catch yourself. So, be aware of that "leaning" tendency, whenever you run.

How do you hold your arms when you run? Some runners

hold the forearm at a 90-degree angle to the upper arm. I think you should drop your forearms even lower. And, as I said, don't hunch up your shoulders. It makes them tense and tired. As you run, check your shoulders occasionally, to be sure they're low and relaxed.

Tuck your chin in so the back of your neck is straight.

In other words, the same straight posture your grammar school teacher tried to teach you is what you want when you run. It keeps your body well-balanced and relaxed, with the minimum of muscle pull and tension.

The Heels Hit First

When you run, you should land on your heels—not on the balls of your feet.

Your heel should hit the ground first—then your arch comes down—then the ball of the foot and toes. You take off from the ball of the foot—and you're into your next step.

Landing on the balls of the feet is bad for you because your calf muscle never gets a chance to stretch. It stays contracted. That's how calf muscles get short and tight. Any kind of running makes your calf muscle shorter and tighter, but running on the balls of the feet makes it worse.

And tight calf muscles are one of the main causes of shin splints, Achilles tendonitis and muscle pulls.

When you're doing speed work or running on hills, you're landing on the balls of the feet. So eliminate this kind of training if you're suffering from any of the injuries I just mentioned.

If you have no injuries, it's okay to run on the balls of the feet for short distances—a short sprint or a little hill work. But when you're doing five, ten, twenty miles a day and you're running on the balls of your feet, you're going to feel a strain in the Achilles tendon.

Right now, whether you're standing or sitting, put your foot through the motion of taking one running step. Put your heel down. Then roll onto the outer side of the foot. Now lift up onto the ball of your foot. That's the right way to run. You have to stop and notice, to appreciate what a complicated job your foot has to do to keep you running. No other foot in the animal kingdom can do it, because no other foot is built like ours.

Our foot is the only one that can be both rigid and flexible. Quadruped runners like dogs and horses have completely rigid feet; all the spring and flexibility come from the legs. Apes' "feet" have all flexibility, with no rigid arch. They really have four hands. Human feet are sometimes rigid and sometimes flexible.

When you run, your weight moves from one part of your foot to another. And it travels along a very definite route. Ideally, your weight goes from the outer side of the heel to the outer side of the arch and then into an area behind the first and second toes. Look at the bottom of your shoes. The wear pattern will tell you the path that your weight is taking.

The first thing that happens in your running step is that the heel gives you a tough, rigid landing platform. Next, the foot muscles move as you go to the arch. The arch flattens out a bit. While your weight is on the arch, you're motionless for a fraction of time. The arch becomes firm and rigid, or else you couldn't stand. You'd have to drop down on your hands, the way our cousins, the apes do.

Next, your weight transfers to the ball of your foot and your toes and you bounce off into your next step. Of course, your legs are providing some of that springing action, too.

I'm describing all this, not just to make you realize what a wonderful mechanism your foot is, but to point out that you shouldn't think your feet are deficient if they get a pain or an injury now and then. I'm surprised we don't get even more injuries than we do. In running, your foot is doing such a complex job, with so many changes in where the weight falls, that almost no foot can do it—thousands of times per run—without showing signs of stress.

Every foot has some little imbalance built into it. When

you run long distances, these imbalances really become evident. And your foot needs help in doing its job—arch supports, strapping, padding, supportive shoes. I want you to appreciate your feet the way I do, and don't get mad at them when they need a little help.

Where Not to Run

The ideal running surface would be a dirt road, or grass, with no incline and no holes. This is the most injury-preventive running environment.

Obviously, you can't always get that. And you don't always need to. But, if you're having pains, problems and injuries, there are certain places you should avoid.

Sand When you run on sand, your heels are sinking in and you're giving an extra pull to the Achilles tendon. So don't do it if you have any calf problems, Achilles problems or shin splints. Also beginning runners should not run on sand because their muscles and tendons are not flexible enough for all that pulling. When you're a beginner, try to run under ideal conditions until your body has built up and stretched out.

Actually, running on sand isn't great for anyone. But it is enjoyable, so if you have no injuries and you really want to run on sand, do it for short distances. Run on the damp, firm sand near the ocean—not on the soft, deep sand.

Hills When you run on hills, you're landing on the ball of your foot and your heel has a longer way to go to reach the ground. You're pulling hard on the Achilles tendon and delivering a harder blow to the ball of the foot. If you're running on a steep hill, your heel may never reach the ground—you're just keeping your calf muscles contracted.

So if you're having trouble with bone bruises in the ball of the foot or Achilles tendonitis or shin splints or runner's knee, don't run on hills until the pain has disappeared—and then go back to hill work slowly.

Pavement   It's difficult not to run on pavement; for most people it's the most available surface. But many parks have some dirt roads you can use. If you have to run on pavement, be sure your shoes have good cushioning; try adding an extra Spenco lining or other lining if you're suffering from impact shock or heel bruise or runner's knee.

Banked Tracks; Roads with an Incline   When you run on an incline, your upper foot is twisting inward with every step. And you're giving yourself one short leg. Both these conditions can lead to injuries. Do run on flat surfaces as much as possible.

The rules for "right running" are simple and common-sensical and they'll become second nature in a short time. As you run, notice other runners' style—it will remind you to check your own posture. Run with other people, and you can watch each other's technique.

Knowing—and practicing—the right way to run can do an awful lot toward keeping you on the road and out of the podiatrist's office.

3
How to Buy Shoes

Personally, I believe you shouldn't have to have an engineering degree to buy a pair of running shoes.

Beginning runners and experienced runners sometimes get very worried about whether they'll pick out the right shoes. They see all the ads in the running magazines with diagrams of the inside of the shoe and special features like impact absorption ratings and varus wedges and rear foot stabilizers and God knows what. Then in the park where all the runners meet and do their stretching, you'll hear all the real pros talking about the different kinds of running shoes. They'll be happy to take a few hours and tell you how they went through seven pairs before they got the right shoes, and how the wrong shoes can give you muscle pulls.

Then they go into the discussions of different kinds of glues to repair their shoes and the would-be runner is about ready to quit, because it seems about as hard to buy a good pair of shoes as it is to buy a reliable car. And the price of making a mistake seems equally disastrous.

Well, there is a lot you can learn about running shoes. A lot of thought goes into their design. And as you become an experienced runner, you'll probably want to learn more about the shoes. Later in this chapter, we'll talk about special problems and advice for more experienced runners.

But you can learn, in about fifteen minutes, how to buy the right running shoes for you. And on page 31, you'll find a checklist you can take with you to the store. It gives you the eight points you have to look for in buying running shoes.

To make sure we were giving you all the information you need, we decided to take Ruth Burr, a new runner, shopping for shoes. So she had the advice of a podiatrist (me) and a shoe expert—Mitch Maslin, owner of the Athletic Attic store on Third Avenue, here in New York. Listen in on our conversation, and you'll have the same experts helping you buy your shoes.

We're sitting in the store with five shelves of shoes in front of us. I take a look at Ruth's feet.

Murray: Ruth, you have fairly narrow feet, and they're bony—not much fat padding. You definitely need shoes with good padding, especially here in the city where you run on paved roads.

Mitch: Yes, padding is one of the most important things about a running shoe for a new runner.

Ruth: Why? Doesn't an experienced runner need padding too? Do your feet change as you run?

Mitch: Well, they may—but the important thing is that your whole body changes as you run and do your stretching exercises. You become stronger and more flexible, so you often don't need so much foot padding to protect you from the shocks and jolts of running.

Murray: That's true. Running is much harder on your body when you're new. It's the beginning runner who gets the aches and pains and muscle pulls. Also, the experienced runner who suddenly tries to run beyond his capacity.

Mitch: More experienced runners often prefer lighter shoes with less cushioning, because it give them better speed. And

some runners just like the feel of the road under their feet.
Murray: But when you're just beginning, you should have
the feel of good cushioning under your feet.
Ruth: That's fine with me. It looks like most of these shoes
have good padding—especially at the heels.
Mitch: Yes, the heel cushioning should be about three-
quarter of an inch thick. The heel is where you really need
cushioning because you land on your heel when you run. And
you land with an impact equal to three times your body
weight. So that can send a real jolt up through your body if
you don't have good thick heels.
Ruth: (*Puts some shoes on*) These shoes really feel good
and comfortable.
Mitch: Yes, your running shoes are probably the most comfortable shoes you've ever put on.
Ruth: Except . . . the arch feels funny. I don't feel such
an arch in my regular shoes.
Mitch: That's probably because your regular shoes aren't
giving you any arch support. You've got to get used to the
feeling of support under your arches.
Ruth: But I don't think I have any arch problems. Does
everyone need arch support for running?
Murray: You certainly need it more than you do in your
regular shoes. Your arch tends to flatten out a bit when you
run—and you don't want it to come down on empty air. You
need some support under it.
Ruth: (*Tries on her street shoes again*) These street shoes
really don't have arch support. My arch doesn't even touch
the shoe, in some spots.
Murray: That's one reason why women's feet are so tired
at the end of the day. Even with not-too-high-heels—like the
street shoes you're wearing—you're sort of standing on the
balls of your feet all day. A lot of your weight is thrown
forward, instead of being evenly distributed.
Ruth: What about people with real arch problems? Will
these running shoes give them enough arch support?
Murray: No, if a person has fallen arches or other problems,

he'll probably need a support made from a mold of his foot.
Ruth: Okay, so the running shoes feel nice and cushiony.
And I can feel the arch support, which I'll get used to. What
else should I look for? What about the sole of the shoe? It's
made sort of like football cleats. What's the purpose of that?
Mitch: Originally, those waffle soles—they're also called
studded soles—were made to give traction on soft cross-
country surfaces—grass, dirt and changing terrain. Today,
when a lot of the running is done in cities, manufacturers
have incorporated more shock-absorbing features in the sole.
They use higher studs, so less of your foot is in contact with
the ground. And they experiment with different materials.
Of course, today's shoes are still good for cross-country runners. They still give good traction.
Ruth: (*Looking at several brands of shoes*) I notice some
of the shoes don't have studs. They just have a sort of herringbone design. Is that for some special road condition?
Mitch: Not really. The herringbone pattern gives you traction, too, as well as cushioning against paved roads. Actually,
for a beginner, the bottom of the shoe is about the last con-
sideration you should think of.
Ruth: A lot of these shoes have stripes along the side of
the sole. Is that just a design?
Mitch: No, that shows you the different layers of the sole.
Look—even in the shoes that don't have colored stripes on
the side of the sole, you can still see the layers. First, on the
bottom, is a layer made of fairly hard rubber with some ability
to absorb shock. This outer sole is made to contact the road
and stand up to the friction and burning of the road.

  Next comes the midsole. This layer has the most shock ab-

MIDSOLE

sorption. Manufacturers are experimenting with the midsole —trying different materials and air pockets and what not. The problem is to give cushioning without making it too soft. A midsole that's too soft is not giving you enough support. It would compress too much, so you'd get too much movement in your foot and leg and knee.

Murray: And that could lead to too much action in the leg muscles—muscle soreness—knee pain.

Mitch: But that's nothing you have to worry about. Most good shoes have midsoles that are both shock-absorbing and firm. Now, as you get into running, and your shoes start wearing out, I want you to keep checking the soles and heels. Especially the heels. Don't let them get too worn. Here's where those colored stripes on the side can help you. You can see when the bottom sole is worn out, because the color of the midsole stripe starts showing through. Don't ever run with the midsoles hitting the ground.

Ruth: The midsoles aren't tough enough for the ground?

Mitch: That's right—they're not made to stand up to the friction of the ground.

Murray: Also, if the heels are worn down, your foot hits the ground at the wrong angle, and this is one of the big causes of muscle pulls and other injuries—especially knee injuries. If you have knee pain, the first thing you should check is heel wear.

Mitch: Later, I'll tell you how to repair worn-down heels and how to care for your running shoes.

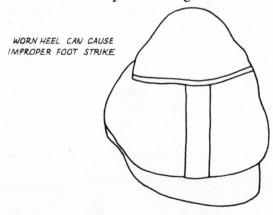

WORN HEEL CAN CAUSE
IMPROPER FOOT STRIKE

Ruth: Okay, so on the outside I can see the bottom sole and the midsole. And inside the shoe is the insole.
Mitch: Right. The insole is designed to be soft and comfortable. They use shock-absorbing material, like the Spenco insole. The insole is also supposed to minimize blisters.
Ruth: Blisters! I got a blister my first day running, in sneakers. I think the sneakers were too tight.
Murray: Let's talk about blisters a minute. You can get blisters from shoes that are too tight or too loose. If your shoes are too loose, your foot will be sliding back and forth, and that friction causes a blister.

Even socks can cause blisters. Nylon socks are abrasive, so be sure you get cotton or woolen socks. Also try to get socks that come in sizes. Those socks that say "one size fits all" can be too tight and cause pressure and interfere with your circulation.

Sometimes the counter of the shoe causes blisters. The counter is the back part of the shoe that wraps around your heel. It's got to be firm, to give support, but because it's firm, it can rub. A counter that's too loose can cause a blister on the heel.
Mitch: That's true, but you have to expect your heel to move a little in the shoe. Sometimes that will cause a blister, especially when you're just breaking in new shoes. That doesn't necessarily mean you've bought the wrong shoes. They just have to be broken in a little.

Also, your skin may be too soft, and then you'll get a blister. Or you may overdo—you run so many miles and there's so much friction on your foot, you get blisters. At the end of the New York City Marathon this year, I guarantee I'll come in with blisters on the bottom of my feet—no matter what shoes I wear.
Murray: If you do get a blister, you can just open it and let the fluid out. Then tape some gauze over it, to protect it. (See page 119 on blisters.) But let's get back to buying shoes now.
Mitch: Right—the next thing I want you to notice is how

the toes fit. Be sure your toes have plenty of room. They shouldn't hit the front of the shoe. Also, don't tie the laces too tightly over the toes, because that can cut off the circulation. Your feet swell as you run. Your foot can expand a full size during a long, hot run.

Murray: Be sure your shoes are long enough to give your toes plenty of room. But your running shoes should fit a bit more snugly, laterally, than your street shoes.

Mitch: Murray, I find a lot of my customers have one foot bigger than the other.

Murray: Yes, most people do, and it's nothing to worry about—unless one foot is a lot larger. In that case you have to fit the larger foot. Then you can put a Spenco insole, or any soft insole, in the other shoe to make it fit.

Ruth: I don't think there's much difference in the sizes of my feet. But I do have narrow feet. Do running shoes come in widths?

Mitch: Some of them do. Also, certain brands tend to be wider or narrower, although there are so many models within each brand that it's hard to make a general rule. I find that Adidas shoes tend to be narrow. Nike and Puma tend to be wide. Brooks shoes seem to be medium. New Balance comes in widths, and so do some other brands.

The thing is, each manufacturer has several models. In a running shoe store, the salesman will be familiar with the different styles, and he can bring out the models that will be best for your foot.

Ruth: I notice some of these shoes are made for women.

Mitch: Yes, they're made on a woman's last. The main difference is that women's shoes are narrower.

Ruth: Wait, my size is six-and-a-half, and you've given me a size seven.

Mitch: Don't worry about the numbers. A lot of people take a larger size in a running shoe. Sometimes they insist on getting their usual size, and they walk out with shoes that are too small for them.

I think it's smart to buy shoes in the afternoon, because

your feet can expand a full size during the day.

Ruth: Let me try a six-and-a-half anyway, since that's my usual size. . . . Mmmm, I guess it is tight—my foot's making the shoe bulge out on the side.

Murray: When that happens, the sides of the shoe can't give your foot the support it needs. That's what happens when you buy a shoe that's too narrow. Your foot won't be stable as you're running, and that can lead to muscle strain and tiredness and injuries. Also, if the shoe is too tight, you'll cut off the circulation and your foot becomes numb.

Ruth: All right, I give up. I'll take a larger size.

Mitch: Now let's check—the toes have enough room. The width is snug but not too tight. The last thing to notice about fit is the heel counter—that's the part that wraps around the heel. The counter should fit snugly, but not be so stiff that it rubs and causes irritation. The counter should be firm enough to hold your heel solidly because a wobbly heel can cause injuries in the lower leg.

Ruth: How can I tell if the counter is firm enough?

Mitch: Just squeeze it—it should feel firm. And, as I said before, don't worry if the counter does cause a blister at first. You have to give it a chance to break in.

While we're looking at the counter, here's something you should check when you buy shoes. Place the shoes on a level surface and look at them from the rear. The counter should sit straight and square on the shoe. Sometimes one of the counters is tilted in, and that could cause a wrong movement in your foot.

Ruth: Okay, so I should check to see that the counter's on straight. Now I have another question about the back of the shoe. Why are they shaped differently from the heels of regular shoes?

Mitch: They're different in two ways. One, a good running shoe will have a flared heel. The heel widens out as it goes toward the ground. This gives you a larger base to land on—because you land on your heel. This larger base makes you more solid and stable. Also, since you're landing on a larger

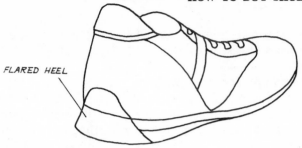

FLARED HEEL

area, you've got more shock-absorbing material underneath you.

Besides being flared, the heels of running shoes are rounded. This lets you hit the ground more smoothly.

Ruth: That makes sense. Now, what about flexibility? All my friends tell me I should be sure I get flexible shoes.

Mitch: That means the shoe should bend at the ball of the foot. Where your foot bends, the shoes should bend easily.

Murray: Your foot bends at a 35-degree angle when you toe off, so your shoe has to bend along with it. If the shoe doesn't bend easily, your muscles are working hard against the shoe. So you get soreness in the shins or the calf muscles or the Achilles tendon.

Mitch: People used to say you should test new shoes on the scale—you should put the toe of the shoe on the scale, then push down on the back of the shoe. And it should take no more than five pounds of pressure to bend the shoe. Well, I really wouldn't worry about that. If you like the shoe in other respects, the flexibility will come as you break them in, and you can help them along. Bend them back and forth several times before you wear them. And don't forget, for every mile of running, each foot is bending eight hundred times. So you're bound to increase the flexibility. You can make cuts along the bottom of the sole—at the ball of the foot—to help them bend more easily.

Murray: Or before you do that, you can try my method. When I have new shoes that are too stiff, I bend them at the ball of the foot, then tape them in that position and leave them that way overnight.

Mitch: I bend my shoes, and put them in a shallow dresser drawer overnight, so they stay bent. That makes them more flexible.

Now let's talk about the weight of the shoe. You hear a lot of talk about this from experienced runners. Racers want the lightest shoes they can get, because every gram of weight can add that much more effort to their run. But, for a beginning runner, a lightweight shoe is not that important. It's much more important for you to have good, solid cushioning under your foot.

Murray: And the heavier you are, the more cushioning you need. A lot of new runners are overweight, so they need extra-solid cushioning and support. In fact, when I get a patient who's overweight and is having problems—like pains in the heel or pains in the hips and spine—caused by the shock of hitting the ground in running—I advise them to wear work shoes, even combat boots. I got this idea from Dr. Schuster. You can't run a marathon in combat boots, but when you're first starting out, they hold you good and firm. They absorb a lot of impact. By the time you're ready to run a marathon, you'll have a lightweight body and you'll feel comfortable in lightweight shoes.

Ruth: You've told me the shoes will change as I break them in. How long does it take to break in new running shoes?

Mitch: I would say two or three weeks of gradual breaking in. I would start by wearing them around the house a few evenings or just wearing them in the street. Then go for a short run. Since you're a new runner, your runs will be short anyway. Then if you wear your running shoes on other occasions—if you just wear them like regular sport shoes— the shoes will break in as you're breaking in—getting used to running.

Murray: I tell my patients never to enter a race in brand new shoes. Your shoes and feet ought to be used to each other before you go into a race together. You should buy new shoes before the old ones are worn out. Then you wear the new shoes for a short run, or wear them every second or third day. Break them in, the way Mitch is saying. So the new shoes are breaking in as the old ones are wearing out. And you never have to race in stiff, unfamiliar shoes.

Ruth: I notice most of these shoes are nylon on the top—part nylon and part leather.

Mitch: Yes, the nylon uppers are good because they don't need breaking in. They're nice and soft the first time you put them on. They cause less friction against your skin. And they're light in weight, so that feels good.

Also, if leather shoes get wet they often stiffen up and crack when they dry. You often go out running on rainy days, so your shoes get wet. Plus, your feet sweat a lot. Then in winter, the salt they throw on the sidewalk can make leather shoes stiff and cracked.

You shouldn't worry about getting your shoes wet, if they have nylon uppers. Just stuff them with newspapers and let them dry. But don't put them near heat. Don't try to dry them in the oven or with a hair dryer. The sole may separate from the rest of the shoe. I wouldn't even put shoes in strong sunlight to dry. Just let them dry at room temperature. They'll probably be dry the next day, and you can flex them a few times and put them right on.

Ruth: Everyone told me that running shoes are so expensive. But really, they're no more expensive than regular street shoes.

Mitch: That's true—and besides, good shoes are really the only "must" equipment in running. It's perfectly okay to run in cheap shorts and a T-shirt. I don't think cutoff jeans make good running shorts, because they're too stiff. Soft nylon shorts are better, but they don't have to be expensive.

Ruth: Anyway, if you wanted to save money on shoes, you could buy cheaper ones, right? In department stores and regular shoe stores.

Mitch: I wouldn't. The companies that make shoes for department stores and regular shoe stores have not been making running shoes for years. They're trying to make quick imitations of real running shoes. But the only thing you can count on is that they're imitating the cosmetics—the colors and styling. You don't know what's gone into the inside of the shoe.

The companies that specialize in running shoes have years and years of experience and testing behind them, and they're constantly working on improving the running shoes. Even when running was not a big fad, Adidas and Nike were making running shoes. Brooks was making sports shoes, twenty or thirty years ago. I would trust the real running shoe companies like these—or basically, the shoes sold in stores that specialize in running equipment.

Ruth: How long do running shoes last?

Mitch: It's very hard to say. Different people wear them out at different rates. Some people are lighter on their feet. Some people drag their feet. The identical brand and model can wear out at different rates, on different runners. You may even find that one of your shoes wears out faster than the other because you come down harder on one side.

Ruth: You told me to be sure the heels don't get worn—so I don't run on the midsoles. What about that stuff people use to mend the soles? Is that any good?

Mitch: Sure, you can get Shoe Goo, or other good glues for just a few dollars and really prolong the life of your shoes. In fact, you should apply this stuff to the heels very frequently to keep them from wearing down. When your heels wear down, your foot is hitting the ground at a bad angle, and that can cause you all sorts of leg and knee and back problems.

I apply glue to my heels every three or four runs, to prevent wear.

Ruth: That sounds like a lot of trouble. Does it take much time?

Mitch: Not much more than squeezing out toothpaste. Squeeze it out and apply a thin coat. You'll get the feel of it—you'll notice that the stuff contracts a bit when it dries. So I bring the material up above the heel a little—knowing it will shrink down as it dries. The salesman in the running shoe store will show you how to use it—or you can just experiment with it yourself.

So that's how Ruth bought her first pair of running shoes. And her experience should give most people all the guidance necessary to buy the proper shoes—whether you're a new runner or an old-timer. In fact, here's a checklist you can take with you to the store:

1. **Cushioning**   Very important. You need about ¾-inch at the heel and good cushioning under the ball of the foot.

2. **Length**   Should be long enough to give toes plenty of room. Toes should not touch the front of the shoe.

3. **Width**   Shoes should feel snug and firm, but should not be so tight that they bulge on the side.

4. **Arch**   Running shoes have good arch support—more than street shoes—and this is a feeling you'll get used to.

5. **Counter**   Should feel firm when you squeeze it. Counter should be set square and straight onto the heel—not tilted.

6. **Heel**   Should be wider at the base than at the top of the shoe. (Flared heel.)

7. **Flexibility**   Shoe should bend easily at the ball of the foot. But flexibility will improve as you wear the shoes.

8. **Comfort**   Shoe should feel good on your foot, even though it may be a bit snugger than your street shoes.

These eight points are all you have to look for—unless you have special problems.

Special Shoe Tips for Special Problems

Overweight Runners   If you're overweight or have a very large frame, you need more cushioning than other people. Buy cushioning liners from the footcare stand in your drugstore, and bring them with you when you're trying on shoes.

Arthritis or Knee Damage   You need extra cushioning too—so follow the procedure given for the heavy runner.

Achilles Tendonitis   You need extra lift in the back of the shoe. Start with heel lifts made of sponge rubber, a ¼-

inch thick, and see if that solves the problem. Then work up to ½-inch or ¾-inch, if necessary. Victex makeup sponges are good, and they come in various thicknesses. Or buy sponge rubber on the foot care stand.

Ankle Sprains and Instability If you tend to turn your ankle frequently and get ankle sprains, you can add something to the outside of your shoe to give you more stability. Read the section on sprained and broken ankles. It gives instructions for your shoemaker, on how to apply a strip of rubber to the outer side of your running shoes. This strip makes it almost impossible for you to turn your ankle and sprain it.

Arch Problems You need special arch support, and a mass-produced shoe isn't designed to give you this. Read the section of this book that describes your problem—it's probably the section called weak foot—for guidance in getting the arch support you need.

Shin Splints Be sure your shoes are flexible. And be sure you've got good heel lift. Try adding heel cushioning, inside the shoe. Be sure the toes are not too loose. If your toes have too much space, they're constantly grabbing, trying to get more stability. But they're grabbing at empty air, and that can cause shin splints.

My friend Mitch Maslin cured his shin splints when he switched to Brooks Vantage shoes. They have thick heel cushioning plus an extra-wide sole. They're wider across the arch and the ball of the foot. I think it was the higher heel that did the trick. Mitch thinks the extra width prevented excess motion in the leg and foot, and that cured the shin splints. Anyway, it worked.

Corns on Top of the Toes; Hammer Toes You need plenty of room in the toe box. You may have to cut slits in your shoes to provide that.

Bunions If you can't get shoes wide enough to keep your bunions comfortable, cut slits in the side of your shoes. Then cover the hole with moleskin, or glue on a piece of nylon, so the bunion doesn't get hurt.

4

The Best Anti-Injury Exercises I've Ever Found

-And The Easiest Way To Do Them

I'm going to let you in on a secret that could cut my practice by a third.

If you do the right exercises and do them regularly, you can avoid most injuries. On the other hand, if you run and don't exercise, you're almost sure to be injured. It's that simple.

Every run you take causes microscopic tears in the muscles, and when these tiny tears repair themselves, they form scar tissue. This scar tissue cannot be flexed or stretched. So every time you run, your muscles are getting tighter and tighter—and less able to stretch. A tight, inflexible muscle is a setup for injury. It can't take the shocks and jolts of running or the constant pulling of a long runner's stride. A tight muscle is one that's ready to be injured.

And, along with these tight muscles, other muscles in your body are left pretty much unexercised by running. This means some of your muscles are very tight while nearby muscles are relatively very soft. That's another setup for injury.

So save yourself some pain and money. Learn a basic group of exercises like the warm-up I'll give you here, or any good, well-balanced set of exercises.

I'm absolutely serious when I tell you that the right exercises can keep you out of the doctor's office. Here's an example. When I first got the idea for this book, I wrote up a couple of sections, including a discussion of Achilles tendonitis. I sent it to St. Martin's Press and the head of the sales force, who is a runner, read the section. He did the exercises. And he cured a case of Achilles tendonitis that had been bothering him for months. And he didn't even have to buy the book!

Here's another story. John Tesh is a TV newsman who runs in the New York City Marathon carrying broadcasting equipment. The marathon isn't tough enough—he has to talk and comment and interview other runners as he goes.

Well, in 1978 John was really suffering from runner's knee and was afraid he couldn't run in the marathon. He came to see me and I taught him exercises (standing leg lifts) to strengthen the quadriceps (thigh) muscles. John ran the marathon and tells everyone it was the exercises that got him through.

So make up your mind that you have to exercise before and after you run. And you might as well find ways to enjoy it, or at least make it a habit.

How much time should you spend exercising? I'd say twenty minutes, minimum—ten minutes before running and ten minutes after. This may sound like a lot if you're a beginner—because you may be running or jogging only twenty minutes. But beginners need the exercises more than anyone else, so don't skimp on them. They're the only way to avoid aches and pains and muscle pulls.

For experienced runners, figure your exercising time should equal one quarter of your running time. So if you run about ninety minutes, exercise a little more than twenty minutes.

Now, which exercises should you do? Which are the most effective for preventing injury?

I treat thousands of runners' injuries a year and usually the treatment involves some exercises. My patients try the exercises and report back to me—so over the years I've found out which exercises work better than others and which can actually cause harm. (I'll mention a couple of those later.) I've refined all these exercises down to a basic group of eight that take ten minutes to do. My patients call them the Weisenfeld Warm-up. They're the most effective exercises I've found for the prevention and treatment of runners' injuries.

Some of the exercises I'll give you here include little variations on exercises you may already know. For instance, you may be doing wall push-ups for your calf muscles. Okay, now add this: After you've finished stretching your leg—stretching it out behind you, knee straight—dip your knee. Keep the heel on the floor. Feel the difference? Now you're stretching the soleus, which is another muscle in the calf that often gets injured.

Or you may be stretching your hamstrings by putting one foot on the table and holding it with your hands. Try this instead: For half of your stretching time, hold your foot with your left hand. For the rest of the time, hold the foot with your right hand. You'll feel the difference—you're reaching different muscles. Doing it this way gives each muscle a better stretch than when you hold your foot with both hands at once.

I've chosen exercises that stretch or strengthen more than one muscle group at a time. So you get more injury-prevention for your effort. And I've found an easier way to do them. Start them in bed. Do the first three exercises in bed, before you get up in the morning. It's like stretching when you first get up. (Be sure you have a firm mattress.)

Then get out of bed and continue stretching and warming up your muscles as you do the last five exercises. Now you're ready for your morning run.

If you take your run in the evening, Bob Glover recommends taking a hot bath before you start exercising—to relax the muscles. If that seems like too much trouble, lie on the floor and do some gentle deep breathing and stretching before your workout. It's very important to be relaxed when you exercise and when you run.

Too many people come in from work full of tension and immediately start forcing their tight muscles to exercise. When they run, they're still tense. This is the way injuries start. If you're tense, relax and breathe a bit before you exercise. And start your run with a long, easy walk.

Do whatever you can to stay relaxed while exercising. Stretch with a slow, relaxed feeling and stretch just to the point where you can feel the muscle stretching—but not hurting. If you stretch too hard, the muscle will resist and contract.

The same rule applies to strengthening exercises. For instance, when you're doing sit-ups, your abdominal muscles should be making an effort, but they should not be hurting. Don't try to do the full number of repetitions I give here, if you're out of condition. Do the exercise a few times and build up slowly.

Another important tip: Never bounce when you exercise. It kills me to see how some people exercise—they bounce as they touch their toes and bounce some more as they bend to the side. It hurts me to watch. Because bouncing signals the muscle to contract, and that's the opposite of what you want.

So don't bounce. Stretch slow and easy.

Another don't: the hurdler's stretch, where you have one leg bent and you're reaching for the other leg. This is a twisting motion, which can always be dangerous. You may twist your bent knee. You may pull the inner thigh muscle.

I don't like bending over and putting the palms of the hands flat on the floor. People often throw their backs out this way. This exercise is sometimes shown with the legs together and sometimes with the legs spread. I don't advise either one.

The exercises I'm giving you here include the basic Weisenfeld Warm-up (eight exercises), plus twelve supplementary exercises. You can add an exercise from the supplementary group if you need it for the treatment of a specific injury.

If you're a new runner, I'd advise you to do the basic

warm-up before and after each run. They are a complete injury-preventive program for the great majority of runners. But, if you have a special problem and you do get an injury, you can add the exercise for the muscle group involved. As you read the section on your injury, it will tell you which exercises to do.

If you're an experienced runner and you have a group of exercises that work for you, stick with them. That's the most important thing—what works for you. But I know that runners are always looking for ways to improve their results—so take a look at these exercises. Try a few and see if they get at muscles you're not reaching now.

The Weisenfeld Warm-up

These can be done in bed, before you get up in the morning.

1. Foot Press Strengthens quadriceps, for treatment of runner's knee. Strengthens anterior leg muscles, for treatment of shin splints.

2. Inner and Outer Thighs Strengthens thigh muscles. For treatment/prevention of runner's knee and groin pull.

3. Knee Press Stretches hamstrings and lower back muscles. For treatment/prevention of hamstring pull and lower back pain.

Now get out of bed and do these.

4. Three-Level Leg Lift Strengthens abdominal and quadriceps muscles. Stretches lower back and hamstring muscles.

5. Wall Pushups Stretches the calf muscle and soleus muscle. For treatment/prevention of Achilles tendonitis, shin splints and muscle pulls.

6. Foot on Table, Knee Up Stretches hamstrings. Prevents hamstring pull.

7. Flying Exercise Relaxes upper back muscles which often tense up during running.

8. Shrugs Relaxes shoulders and upper back muscles.

Foot Press   **Inner Thighs**

Foot Press Strengthens quadriceps (thigh) muscles, for treatment/prevention of runner's knee. Strengthens anterior leg muscles, for treatment of shin splints.

Can be done lying down or sitting in a chair. Put your right foot on top of your left foot. Your lower foot tries to pull toward your body as your upper foot pushes it away from the body. Hold for ten seconds. Now switch feet—put the left foot on top of the right foot, and push/pull for ten seconds. This equals one set. Do five sets.

Inner and Outer Thighs The turned-out position strengthens the outer thigh muscles—for treatment/prevention of runner's knee.

The turned-in position strengthens the inner thigh muscles—for treatment/prevention of groin pull.

Can be done lying down or sitting in a chair. Stretch both legs out—knees straight, feet flexed. (Toes pointed toward knees.) Tighten your thigh muscles. Now turn your feet out as far as you can and hold ten seconds. Then turn your feet in as far as you can and hold ten seconds. Keep thigh muscles tight throughout exercise.

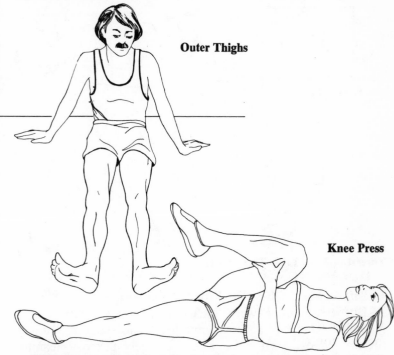

Outer Thighs

Knee Press

Knee Press   Stretches the hamstring muscles and the lower back muscles. For treatment/prevention of hamstring pull and lower back pain.

Lie on your back. Put your hands under one knee and pull your knee to your chest. Hold ten seconds. Relax.

Repeat with other leg. Do each leg five times, alternating legs. Do not wrap your arms around the outside of your knee.

Three-Level Leg Lift   Levels one and two strengthen the abdominal and quadriceps muscles. Level three stretches the lower back and the hamstring muscles.

Lie on your back, legs straight, knees firm but not locked. The small of your back should touch the floor. If it doesn't, put your hands under your buttocks.

Three-Level Leg Lift—First and Second Levels

Three-Level Leg Lift—Third Level

1. Lift legs six inches. Hold for five seconds.
2. Lift legs another twelve inches. Hold five seconds.
3. Swing your legs up over your head until your feet touch the floor above your head. Keep your feet flexed—meaning the toes pointing toward the knees. If you can't get your feet all the way to the floor, go as far as you can without strain, keeping your feet flexed. Hold five seconds.

The above equals one set. Do five to ten sets.

Wall Pushups   Stretches the calf muscle and the soleus muscle. For treatment/prevention of Achilles tendonitis, shin splints and muscle pulls. "Wall Pushups" is the name most people use for this exercise; but don't confuse it with "floor pushups." You should not pump your arms during this exercise. Just take a position and hold it.

Stand facing the wall—about two feet away from the wall. Rest palms of hands against wall. Keep both feet pointing straight ahead. Slide one foot back, with the knee straight, until you feel a burning or pulling sensation at the upper part of the calf. Your heel stays flat on the floor. This stretches the calf muscle. Hold ten seconds. After ten seconds, bend the knee of the back leg and hold five seconds. This stretches the soleus, which is another calf muscle. Now switch legs and repeat.

Do each leg five times, alternating legs.

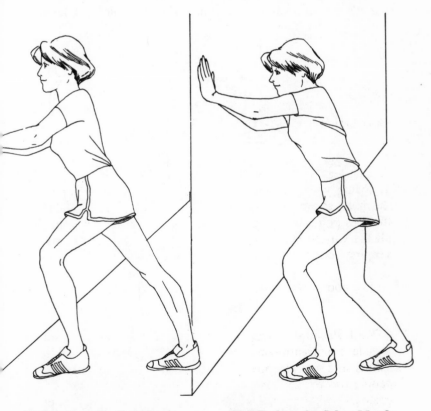

Wall Pushups for Calf Muscle   **Wall Pushups for Soleus Muscle**

Foot on Table, Knee Up   Stretches hamstring muscles, for treatment/prevention of hamstring pull.

Stand in front of a table and put one foot on the table, knee facing up. Keep both knees straight. Bend over and hold the foot that's on the table with your right hand. Bring your nose as close to your knee as possible. Don't force it. Don't strain to make your nose touch your knee. Hold ten seconds.

Now your right hand lets go of your foot, and your left hand holds it. This stretches different leg muscles. Hold ten seconds. Repeat with the other leg.

Stretch each leg five times, alternating legs.

If it's too difficult to put your leg on a table, put it on a chair.

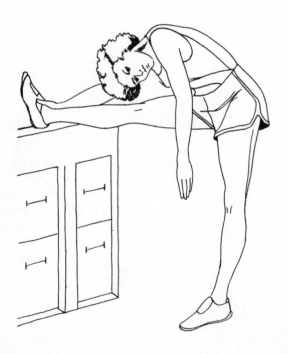

Foot on Table, Knee Up

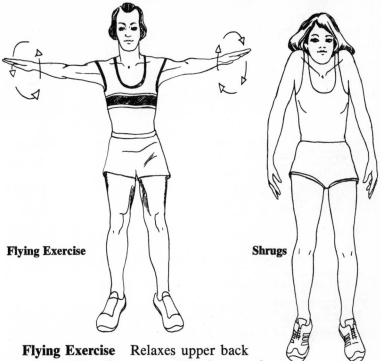

Flying Exercise

Shrugs

Flying Exercise   Relaxes upper back
muscles which often tense up during running.

Hold your arms out straight, shoulder level.

Make ten circles forward and ten circles backward.

This exercise is also a favorite with skiers—only you make
bigger circles. On a freezing day when you can't keep your
fingers warm, stop on the side of the slope (out of traffic) and
do the Flying Exercise. It brings blood to your fingers and
warms them up.

Shrugs   Relaxes shoulders and upper back muscles.

Curl your shoulders down and forward, as if you're trying
to make them touch each other in front. Next, lift your shoulders up toward your ears. Then stretch them way down in
back, as if the two shoulder blades could touch.

Then back up to the ears, and hunched forward again. This
equals one.

Do ten times.

Supplementary Exercises for Particular Muscle Groups

Bent-Leg Sit-Ups   Strengthens abdominals.
Knee Lifts   Strengthens lower back and abdominal muscles.
Hip Rolls   Strengthens lower back and abdominal muscles.
Furniture Lift   Strengthens anterior leg muscles and quadriceps.
Standing Leg Lifts   Strengthens quadriceps.
Weighted Leg Extensions   Stretches hamstrings.
Squats   Stretches Achilles tendons, adductor muscles, lower back muscles
Butterfly   Stretches adductor muscles.
Inner Thigh Stretch   Stretches adductor muscles.
Inner Thigh Lift   Strengthens adductor muscles.
Foot on Table, Knee Forward   Stretches inner thigh muscles.

Bent-Leg Sit-Ups   Strengthens abdominals—for prevention/treatment of lower back pain.

Lie on the floor, knees bent, feet flat on floor. Put your hands behind your head and sit up. Exhale and press in your stomach as you sit up. Inhale as you go down.

Start with five situps and work up to twenty per day.

If you can't sit up while holding your hands behind your head, put your hands on your thighs. As you sit up, your hands move up toward your knees.

Do not jerk your body up. Put your chin on your chest and curl your spine up off the floor.

If you're a beginner, anchor your feet under a piece of furniture. Don't try to sit up all the way. Just go as far as you can without strain.

Another don't: Don't stretch your hands up over your head while doing sit-ups. I've seen people do this, and they fling their arms forward, using the force to help them sit up. When you do this, you're jerking your body up instead of curling it up smoothly. This jerky action leads to muscle tension.

Bent-Leg Situps

Knee Lifts   Strengthens lower back and abdominal muscles. For treatment/prevention of lower back pain.

Lie on your back, arms straight down at your sides. Pull your knees up to your chest, then slowly lower your feet back down again.

Do ten lifts.

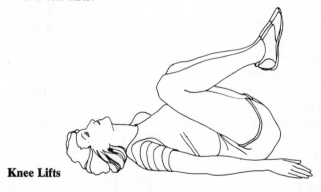

Knee Lifts

Hip Rolls   Strengthens lower back and abdominal muscles. For treatment/prevention of lower back pain.

Lie on your back, arms straight out at shoulder level. Pull

your knees up to your chest. Now roll your knees over to the right side—then back up to center—then over to the left. As much as possible, move only below the waist, not above. Keep the upper back flat on the floor.

Do ten times.

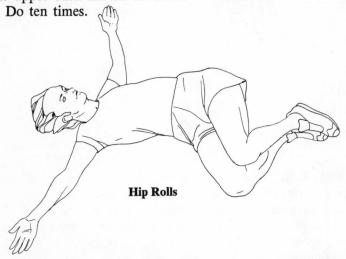

Hip Rolls

Furniture Lift   Strengthens anterior leg muscles. For prevention/treatment of shin splints, Achilles tendonitis and pulls in the calf muscle and soleus muscle. Also strengthens quadriceps.

Tuck your toes under a desk or couch and try to lift it with your toes. Your knees can be straight or bent. Hold ten seconds, then relax.

Do ten lifts. Also, you can do this while talking to boring people, or waiting for someone to answer the phone.

Standing Leg Lifts   Strengthens quadriceps. For prevention/treatment of runner's knee.

Stand with your back against the wall. Lift your leg as high as you can, holding your knee straight. Hold for the count of five. Now bend your knee to relax for the count of five. Then straighten the leg again.

Do one leg five times. Then do the other leg. Start by holding your leg straight for the count of five. Increase till you

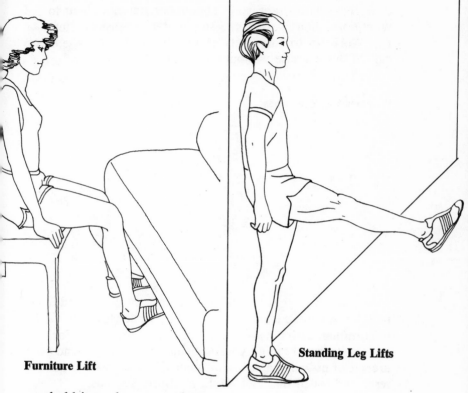

Furniture Lift

Standing Leg Lifts

can hold it to the count of ten.

Weighted Leg Extensions   Stretches and strengthens the hamstring muscles. For treatment/prevention of hamstring pull.

Attach a one-pound weight to each ankle. Lie on the floor, arms at your sides. Your knees are bent, feet flat on floor. Stretch your right leg up as straight as you can. Then put your foot back on the floor. Repeat ten times. Now repeat with your other leg.

Your aim is to straighten your leg so it's almost at a 90-degree angle to the floor. If you have hamstring pull, you will not be able to straighten it completely. Just stretch it as far as you can without causing pain. Do not extend both legs at once, or you'll strain your abdominal muscles. Number of repetitions: Start with three sets of ten extensions for each leg. Work up to three sets of twenty extensions. Beginners can do this exercise without the weights.

Weighted Leg Extensions

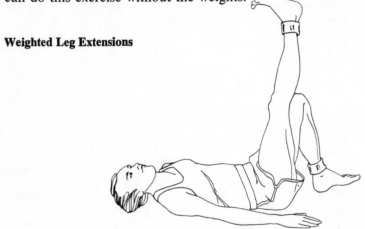

Squats Stretches Achilles tendons. Stretches adductor muscles, for treatment of groin pull. Stretches lower back, for treatment of lower back pain.

Squat down, keeping your heels flat on the floor. Your feet are shoulder-width apart, and pointed out slightly. Bend forward and touch the floor. Hold for thirty seconds.

If your leg muscles and/or Achilles tendons are very tight, you may have trouble keeping your heels on the floor. In this case, put your hands on the wall behind you.

Butterfly Stretches adductor muscles. For prevention/ treatment of groin pull.

Sit with the soles of your feet together. Bring your feet as close to your body as possible. Hold your ankles. Put your elbows on the inner side of the knees. Use your elbows to push your knees down toward the floor. Careful—only to point of stretch, not pain.

Hold ten seconds, then relax. Do five times.

Inner Thigh Stretch Stretches adductor muscles. For prevention/treatment of groin pull.

Squats   **Butterfly**

Stand with your feet slightly wider than hip width. Your left foot points forward and your right foot points toward the side. Bend your right knee and put your weight on your right foot. Hold ten seconds. Now do the other leg: point the right foot forward and the left foot toward the side. Bend your left knee and put your weight on your left foot.

This equals one set. Do five sets.

Inner Thigh Lift   Strengthens adductor muscles. For prevention/treatment of groin pull.

Position: Lie on your right side with your right hand supporting your head. Your left hand is on the floor in front of you, for support. Your left foot is flat on the floor, in front of your right leg. Your right leg should be slightly in front of your body.

Flex your right foot—so the toe points up toward the knee. Keep the knee firm and straight throughout this exercise.

Action: Lift the right leg as high as you can, then lower. Start with five or ten repetitions and work up to twenty. When you lower the leg each time, do not touch the floor with your foot, and do not relax your leg. Keep it firm throughout the exercise.

This can also be done with a one-pound weight on your ankle.

Now turn on your left side and repeat with the left leg.

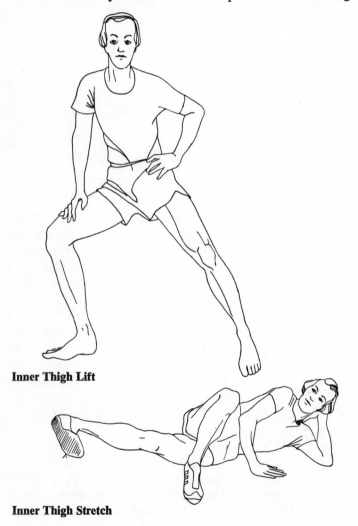

Inner Thigh Lift

Inner Thigh Stretch

Foot on Table, Knee Forward   Stretches inner thigh muscles. For treatment/prevention of groin pull. Stand in front of a table. Put one leg on the table. Both legs should be straight. Do not turn to face your leg. You should face forward, and your knees should face forward. Hold 10 seconds. This equals one set. Do five sets.

As you become more flexible, bend sideways to touch the leg that's on the table.

If it's too difficult at first to put your foot on the table, put it on a chair.

Foot on Table, Knee Forward

5

How to Be Your Own Podiatrist

-And How To Choose a Podiatrist If You Need One

Runners are not passive patients.

One day my friend and patient, Hans Hartmann, walked into my office. I had made some orthotics for Hans about six months earlier, to correct an imbalance that was causing him some ankle pain.

On this day, Hans was carrying the orthotics—but I could hardly recognize them. He had stuck bits of tape and felt and foam rubber on them to thicken them in some spots. Then he had sanded down the orthotics in other places. They were a real mess.

"Here," he said. "Now these orthotics are perfect. Can you duplicate them?" So I duplicated them, and he's been running happily on them ever since. In fact, Hans told me that if he runs for any long period without the orthotics, he feels the ankle pain returning.

Any doctor involved in treating athletes has to take his patients in as partners—because sports medicine is a new science that we're all learning as we go along. Runners, especially, have to become their own doctors to some extent—because your body changes as you run and as you increase your mileage. So if you didn't learn how to take care of yourself, you'd have to reserve a permanent seat in the podiatrist's office.

My patients have learned to become their own podiatrists. (Of course, they call me in for consultation in emergencies.) So let me give you some guidance on how you can do the same.

Naturally, if you do suffer an injury, this book can tell you how to treat it. But "injury fixing" is not the best approach to sports medicine. To take good care of yourself, you need an educated awareness of your body. You need a basic knowledge of the podiatrist's first aid procedures and the tools of first aid. You should know how to take care of your feet from day-to-day and how to keep yourself fit when injuries keep you from running. And you should know how to choose a podiatrist, if you do need one.

Here's some guidance on gaining these skills.

How to Diagnose Your Problem

You've got to be something of a medical detective to find the causes of many injuries. And since you, the athlete, are the eyewitness to the crime, you've got to become an expert at noticing what's going on in your body and in your surroundings.

George Sheehan tells of a swimmer who was beached because of "asthma," until he noticed that it was only in a certain pool that the asthma occurred. It turned out he was allergic to the chemicals in that pool.

One of my patients noticed that changing his shoes cured his shin splints. Mitch had been suffering with shin splints for weeks and we had tried everything. I loaned him my ultrasound machine and gave him heel pads and he did stretching exercises and tried whirlpool baths. Nothing worked.

Then he happened to try a different pair of shoes, and the shin splints went away. One night, when he had his seven pair of shoes turned upside down for repairing, he noticed that the new shoes had much wider soles than the others and thicker heels. So that's what did the trick.

In fact, your shoes can tell you a lot about how you run and why you get injured. Whenever a new patient phones for an appointment, I tell him to bring in some worn running shoes for me to look at.

Look at Your Shoes to See How You Run

The wear pattern on the soles of your shoes shows you how you run. Or, to put it differently, how your weight is transferred from point to point along your foot.

1. A shoe with a normal wear pattern shows that you land on the outer side of your heel. Then your weight moves quickly along the outer side of your foot (not causing much noticeable wear). Now your weight transfers to an area between the first and second metatarsal heads. You can see the wear spot—just behind the first and second toe. This is where you should be taking off into your next step. Fast runners will have a third wear spot at the tip of the shoe, because this is where they take off.
2. Look at the wear pattern for pronation. You get this when you have fallen arches (weak foot). Your arches are weak, so too much of your weight falls toward the inner side of the foot—and that's where you see a big wear spot. You're subject to pains in the arch, leg pains and back pains.
3. In the wear pattern for supination, you can see that too much of the body weight falls toward the outer side of the foot. In this case, your feet don't turn in properly. It's the opposite of pronation. If your feet supinate, you may get some knee trouble.
4. If you have a wear spot behind the big toe, you probably

have bony feet. Your first metatarsal head sticks out, and you may get a bone bruise here (sesamoiditis).

5. If your shoes show excessive wear behind the second and third toes, you probably have corns or calluses in that spot. Too much weight is going there. You have a depressed metatarsal arch.

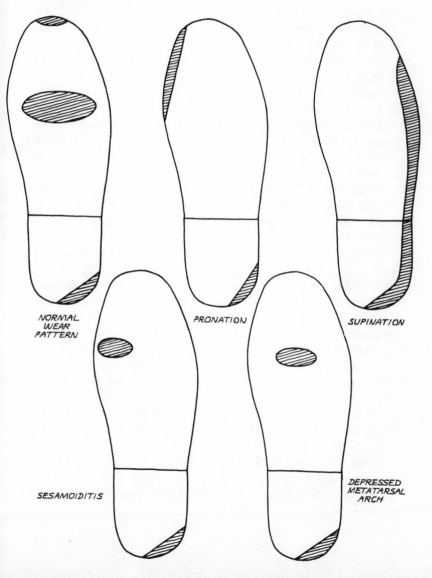

NORMAL
WEAR
PATTERN

PRONATION

SUPINATION

SESAMOIDITIS

DEPRESSED
METATARSAL
ARCH

So pay attention to your shoes and how you run and where you run. Your runner's log is a good way to keep track of these things. In your journal, record your daily mileage and speed. Note how much of the time you're doing hill work. If you ran on an indoor track—a banked track—write that down. If you ran on sand, write that down. Make a note on the weather if it's noticeably hot, cold or rainy—or if the streets are slippery after rain or snow. Note whether you had to push yourself.

Frank Handelman is a patient whose logbook solved the mystery of recurrent injuries he kept getting in the fall.

Frank had been running for years, through high school and college. He always ran hard but never pushed himself, and he almost never had an injury. Now Frank is in his late twenties, working as an attorney and still running steadily. But the big difference is that almost every September, he gets an injury.

In the fall of '75, he got a blister that led to blood poisoning. In the fall of '76, he got tendonitis. In the fall of '77, he got sciatica. In the fall of '79, he broke the big toe on the right foot.

Frank's journal showed him that his right leg had been feeling sore for weeks before the sciatica developed. It also showed him that every summer he was pushing to peak for a big race in August. He was feeling tired and jotting that down in the log book. But he trained hard, in spite of the fatigue. Frank kept making good personal records in that August race and then injuring himself in September.

So make notes how you feel, and how much you run.

If you do get an injury—check and see what you did differently the few days before the injury. If you have shin splints, maybe you were running on a banked road—with the same foot continually on the curb side. Were you doing a lot of hill work or speed work or *fartlek*?

Were you running with someone else? If so, one of you probably had to change stride or run faster than usual. Or, you kept turning your head to talk to the person next to you or behind you. In that case, your foot was hitting the ground at a different angle.

Note when you get a pain, and when it's at its worst. If you have muscle pains during a morning run but not during an afternoon run, you may simply need more warming up.

If you get knee pain as soon as you start running, there's probably something wrong with the knee itself. If the knee pain comes after you've been running a few miles, it's probably a foot imbalance that's causing the wrong movement in the knee—and therefore the pain.

Check your logbook and see how much you were running and where you were running for the days previous to the start of the problem. You may find you've been increasing your mileage too quickly.

If you're trying a new exercise, put that in your journal.

Another way to learn about your own running habits is to have an experienced runner observe your style. Someone else can notice that you're turning your toes in too much or hunching up your shoulders or leaning forward.

Look for symptoms of overstress. For instance:

• Tiredness without being able to sleep.

• Colds, sore throat, fever blisters—any indications of lowered general resistance.

• Lack of enthusiasm for the run. This often comes the day after you've had a terrific, hard, energy-filled run. Along with this lack of enthusiasm comes a lack of interest in your work and everything else you're doing. Jobs that seem challenging and fun when you're feeling good seem just too much trouble when you've been putting too much energy into your running.

If you do get an injury, review what went on the last few days before it happened—and the last few weeks. Question yourself about your running the way a doctor would, if you went to him for treatment. Discuss the injury with a running friend—he may think of more questions to ask. This will give you a clue as to what started the problem.

As you advance in running, you'll find yourself more and more involved in observing how your body ticks. You don't have to drive yourself crazy noticing every detail of your run. Just be an interested observer and you'll learn a lot about what makes your body hurt, and what keeps it healthy.

Your Runner's Medicine Chest

Here are some of the tools and tapes that podiatrists and runners use. Some, you'll want to buy and keep handy. Others, you may not buy right away, but I'd like you to know about them in case you ever do need them.

• Zonis Tape. A porous tape that's very protective. Runners wrap it around an area that's prone to blistering. Baseball players use it on their hands.

• Elastoplast. An elasticized adhesive tape. Many drugstores carry it, or your druggist can order it for you. Comes in one-inch, two-inch and three-inch widths. I use it for the Arch-Supporting Strapping given in the chapter on weak foot. It's good for taping down the cushioning and pads you put on your feet. Ordinary tape sometimes pulls loose when you run or pulls on your skin until the skin tears. Elastoplast stretches as your foot moves, and your padding stays in place. You can wear it in the shower—it gets wet and then dries off again.

• One-inch adhesive tape. I use it to secure the edges of the Elastoplast in the Arch-Supporting Strapping.

• I don't use Band-Aids, because they're plastic coated or lined with Telfa. Telfa and plastic don't allow the escape of liquids from a wound, so a wet wound becomes macerated and doesn't heal quickly.

• Gauze. Keep squares of gauze handy. When you have a blister you've just opened, clean it with an antiseptic, then cover it loosely with gauze. Tape down the edges of the gauze.

• Antiseptic. I like Betadine as well as anything. You can buy it without prescription. I also use Gentian Violet. Ask your podiatrist or other doctor to give you a prescription for 2 percent Gentian Violet, aqueous solution. The aqueous solution keeps it from burning. Or you can buy 1 percent

Gentian Violet without a prescription. Gentian Violet is an antiseptic, a drying agent and a mild fungicide. It's good for blisters and athlete's foot between the toes.

• Pain killers. Use aspirin if you're not allergic to it and don't have ulcers. Get buffered aspirin, so it won't upset your stomach. Ecotrin is a special coated aspirin that releases in the small intestine, so it doesn't cause stomach troubles. Ascriptin is aspirin with Maalox in it, so it coats your stomach to prevent upsets.

Now, here's a warning I give frequently in this book, but I'll give it again here, because it's important. Take aspirin with your meals and at bedtime. Never take pain killers before going out to run, because they mask pain, and pain is a symptom. It's better for you to know that something's going wrong while it's happening. Otherwise, you'll keep running and with every step you're making the problem worse. In the end, it takes longer to heal and you've lost more running time than if you had stopped running when you first felt the pain.

• Emery board for smoothing down corns and calluses. I don't recommend cutting corns with a razor blade, but it's helpful to smooth a corn down a bit with an emery board. You'll break the continuity of the dead skin and restore some elasticity to the skin. By filing the corn a bit, you're making it smaller. That means your shoe won't be so tight, and there'll be less pressure on the corn. If the pressure is taken off long enough, the corn will disappear.

• Doughnut pads for corns are fine. But don't use corn drops. And don't use corn pads impregnated with corn drops. Corn drops are salicylic acid, and it can burn good skin as well as the dead skin. It's dangerous for diabetics and other people with impaired circulation; it's dangerous for everyone.

• Lamb's wool. Curity Brand is a good one. Get the silky kind, not the uncarded lamb's wool. Lamb's wool is good for wrapping around toes that have corns—especially if the corn is on the tip of the toe or the top of the toe. It protects the whole area from pressure—more effectively than aperture pads. Wrap it around toes that are subject to blisters.

• Moleskin. Very handy for cutting out made-to-order cushioning. It's cushioned on one side and adhesive on the other. You can cut out different shapes to put behind the metatarsal heads or the ball of the foot or wherever you need them. Overlap them, double them, quadruple them—make them as thick as you want. You can roll moleskin into sticks to put under the crest of the toes where that's called for.

• Adhesive felt. Use the same way as moleskin. It's thicker than moleskin. You can double and triple the felt, cut holes in it. Trim and taper the edges so it doesn't feel like you're standing on a bump.

• Dr. Scholl's heel pads are good—for the heels as well as other parts of the foot. They can be cut and shaped to fit different parts of the foot. These heel pads are foam rubber that's covered with plastic, so they stay neater than plain foam rubber. Foam rubber sometimes gets messy—covered with tape and sweat.

• Victex Makeup Sponges. You can buy these in Woolworth's or the drugstore. They come in ½-inch and ¾-inch thickness. I like them for heel pads. I find they're just the right texture—just soft enough and just firm enough. I think the stock of Victex must have gone up since I started recommending them and I don't even own stock. One of my patients buys them by the gross. He has to wear heel pads all the time —so this way he always has fresh ones when the old ones get grubby.

• Sponge rubber metatarsal pads and cookies—you can buy these from the shoemaker. Put them in your shoe if you need some arch support. Sometimes these do the trick, and you don't even have to buy a full arch support. They're good for women, because you can put them in a high-heeled shoe, which you can't do with a regular arch support.

• Ice packs you can put in your freezer and use for inflamed Achilles tendons, runner's knees, sprained ankle or other inflamed areas. You can buy these in your runner's store.

First Aid Techniques for the Majority
of Runners' Injuries

Basic first aid for many pains and injuries includes one or more of these tools:
- ice
- elevation
- aspirin
- heat

Ice is the first thing you should use for inflammation and for muscles in spasm. You can buy an ice bag in the runners' store, and keep it in the refrigerator. Or make one by putting cubes in a plastic bag and closing the top with a twist tie.

Inflammation You know an area is inflamed if it feels warm to the touch. If your right ankle has some inflammation, it will feel warmer than your left ankle. Other symptoms of inflammation are redness, swelling, pain and limitation of movement.

Runners often get inflamed ankles, tendons, muscles and knees—and ice will help all of these. Painful heel spurs also respond to ice.

For inflammation, you should use aspirin and ice first (and elevation, where appropriate). Use the ice right after your run. In some cases heat can be used later in the day—a heating pad or hot bath. Here are some specifics.

For a sprained ankle, wrap the area in an ice pack and put the foot on a chair. Continue ice treatments—ten minutes on, ten minutes off—for the first twenty-four hours. Also keep the foot elevated, for the first twenty-four hours. Put a couple of pillows under it when you go to bed.

For knee pain, wrap the knee in an ice pack after running —ten minutes on, ten minutes off, then repeat. A heating pad can be used in the evening. Set it on low, never on high.

For hamstring pull, ice the hamstrings for a half hour after running. Dr. Seymour Goldstein, an excellent runner's chiropractor, advises icing hamstrings a half hour before running, too; but I personally don't recommend using ice before running.

For pain in the heel, caused by heel spur or bruising of the bone, put an ice pack in a basin and rest your heels on that. Leave your feet on ice fifteen minutes—then off fifteen minutes—then repeat.

For pain on the arches or the heads of the metatarsal bones (where the toes connect to the metatarsals), rest the feet on an ice bag, fifteen minutes on—fifteen minutes off—then repeat.

For Achilles tendonitis, wrap the ice bags around the inflamed area for fifteen minutes on. Later in the evening, use the heating pad (on low) to bring blood to the area and promote healing.

For painful muscles after a run, apply an ice pack for ten minutes. Do this before attempting massage. Ice reduces inflammation, stops swelling, and anesthetizes the area. When the pain is diminished, the runner calms down—and that's very important to someone who's exhausted and hurting from a long hard race.

Aspirin—for any of these inflammations, take two aspirins at each meal and two at bedtime—unless you have an ulcer or other reason for not taking aspirin.

Relax a strained muscle before you stretch it. If you have a tight, strained muscle or tendon, you know it has to be stretched. But if it's actually painful—not just tight—wait a few days and let it relax. This means don't stretch and don't run for a few days. Then start your stretching exercises. Meanwhile, you can use a heating pad and hot baths to help your muscles and tendons relax.

Recovering from a big race. The day after a marathon— or any big race—take a few walks, to bring blood to the tight, tired muscles and help the healing process. And do some slow, easy stretching.

Basic Foot Maintenance

Use talcum powder between your toes to absorb moisture and prevent cracking. Talcum powder also reduces friction, so it's a protection against blisters.

In fall and winter, put cream on your heels to prevent cracking. Cracked skin on the heels can be very painful. All creams are about equally good. I suggest Crisco or Spry—they're cheap and they're as effective as any hand cream.

Keep your toenails cut short—long nails can jam into the front of your shoe as you run downhill. This causes black toenail or ingrown toenail. Cut the nails straight across, not curved, to prevent ingrown toenail.

Rub corns and calluses with an emery board to reduce them. It's much more effective than a pumice stone. Very thick calluses have to be removed by the podiatrist.

Alternate Exercises—When You Can't Run

If you're injured, it may console you to know that athletes heal faster than sedentary people because they have better circulation. Nutrients and healing agents are delivered faster to the site of the injury. Also, athletes have better musculature. So, if you've got a foot or leg injury, your muscles do a better job of milking the fluids up out of the swollen area.

It's very important to find some alternate exercise when you can't run. Otherwise, you'll lose endurance quickly. And emotionally, you'll be impossible to live with.

The exercise I don't recommend is jumping rope. What I do recommend is swimming, water exercises, bike riding, stretching and weight work for the upper body.

I don't like jumping rope because you're constantly landing on the balls of your feet and causing a lot of trauma. Jumping on the balls of your feet can cause Achilles tendonitis or shin splints. If you insist on jumping, use a padded mat.

Swimming is an excellent indoor or outdoor exercise. You can keep your muscles and heart in shape, without putting weight on your legs. In terms of aerobic benefit, one mile of swimming equals four miles of running.

Swimming the crawl develops the arms and chest, and that's something many runners need to work on.

Do straight swimming to keep up your cardiovascular fitness. And try a few fun exercises.

• Put a spare tire under your arm pits, and "jog" in the water. This exercises your leg muscles without strain.

• Put flippers on your feet and swim. Good exercise for the quadriceps.

• Do the frog kick. Relieves pain of the outer hip, which occurs either at leg joint or a bit higher, up toward the hip bone.

• Do stretching exercises in the water. Hold onto the side of the pool with both hands. Put your feet flat against the side of the pool and stretch.

Riding a bike is less effective aerobically than swimming or running, but it can keep your leg muscles toned up.

Weight work is good for developing the chest, arms and upper back. One of my patients, Molly Colgan, found that her upper back got tired on long runs, so she started working with weights. Molly just finished her fifth marathon, and she feels the weight work has increased her endurance.

How to Choose a Podiatrist When You Need One

I've given this a lot of thought, and I think the best way is what you'd do on your own—ask other runners. There is an Academy of Podiatric Sports Medicine that podiatrists can join, but all it means is that they've sent in their entry fee and application. A Fellow or Diplomate, however, has qualified by being tested. So I think the best thing you can do is go on the recommendation of other runners.

There are a lot of good podiatrists who don't deal with runners; so they don't learn enough about what happens to the foot in motion. A podiatrist who works with athletes learns something new every day. Before and after a marathon —or any big race—his office is filled with runners bringing him new problems and new information. That's the sort of podiatrist who's likely to know how to solve your problem.

Ask the other runners at your local "Y" or at the running store, or phone your Road Runners' Club.

How much can a podiatrist help you?

I tell my patients that I'm successful about 80 percent of the time. I don't think anyone can actually guarantee success, because every body is different. Also, some types of injuries respond better than others. Some of the injuries we have the best results with are heel spurs, runner's knee, and posterior tibial shin splints. Some problems that we don't always succeed with are groin pull and outer hip pain.

Very often your podiatrist will send you to another specialist—a chiropractor, osteopath or orthopedist. Muscle injuries sometimes need a lot of work and patience and a variety of approaches. But whatever your problem is, it can usually be helped by the teamwork of the right doctor and a knowledgeable, persistent patient.

Then, if all else fails, there's the last resort—try cutting down on your mileage.

6

The Difference Between Hard Orthotics and Soft Orthotics

Patients often ask me why I use "soft" orthotics instead of the "hard" (plastic or metal) orthotics that some podiatrists use.

If you've chosen a podiatrist—probably on the recommendation of other runners who've had success with him—I think you should trust his judgment. But I find that runners are very involved patients; they like to know what's going on, and why I'm using this treatment instead of some other one.

A lot of my patients are physicians and enjoy discussing different forms of treatment. But, no matter what line of work you're in, you're certainly concerned with your own injury and what's being done for it.

So, for your information, I'll tell you some of the differences between hard and soft orthotics; and why I almost always use the soft orthotics.

Hard orthotics are made of molded plastic or hard-hammered steel.

Soft orthotics are made of rigid leather bonded to a mixture of rubber and wood flour. Because they're made of leather, dogs eat soft orthotics. Also, greasy substances like Vaseline separate the leather tops from the bottoms. So don't put greasy ointments on your feet when you wear soft orthotics.

Both types of orthotics are made to a mold of your foot. Here are some differences in how they work.

1. Hard orthotics do not cover the entire bottom of your foot. They stop behind the metatarsal heads (the ball of the foot). They give less control to problems in the forefoot.

For instance, your doctor may decide that the front of your foot needs to be tilted inward by a few degrees. Okay. He has an orthotic made with a wedge to tilt your foot inward.

But, if you get a plastic orthotic, which stops at the ball of the foot, your forefoot will not be tilted into the exact degree it needs. The soft tissue in the ball of your foot absorbs some of the tilt.

Another forefoot problem you may have is Morton's foot (your big toe is shorter than your second toe). To correct this problem, your podiatrist can prescribe a soft orthotic that raises the head of the first metatarsal and thereby gives better forefoot control. But a hard orthotic only raises the area behind the first metatarsal head, so you get less control.

2. Plastic orthotics can be compressed at the arch just by pressing on them with your thumb. Then the heel tilts up. Soft orthotics stay firm when you press on the arch. The heel doesn't tilt up.

What does this mean when you're running? If the arch is flattening, and the heel is tilting up, your foot may be pronating—turning inward. Excessive pronation is one of the problems we're usually trying to correct. It's a cause of many runner's injuries.

3. Now, the heel area. Your foot may need to be tilted inward or outward at the heel. We do this by putting a wedge on the bottom of the orthotics. In a soft orthotic, the wedge presses up through the leather, and your heel tilts the way it should.

But a plastic orthotic is so rigid the wedge does not press up, and your heel is not tilted properly.

4. I can fix and adjust a soft orthotic right in the office. A plastic orthotic has to be sent back to the laboratory, and you have to wait ten days.

Let me explain how this works. When you need orthotics, your doctor tests and measures your feet, makes a mold of your foot, and sends it to the lab with instructions. About ten days later, the orthotics come back, and you put them in your shoes and go out and run.

Then you start phoning your doctor's office and complaining. The arch is too high or not high enough; you need more cushioning here or less tilt there. For two weeks the doctor tells you to hang in and keep running to break in the device.

After two weeks, he wants to hear your complaints. Now you know what really needs adjustment. With soft orthotics, the doctor can sand a little material off the bottom, or glue a little on, and you're off and running. You may have to come back two or three times, for little adjustments. When you're done, you've got an orthotic device that's truly custom-made to your foot and your way of running.

This convenience is a big reason why many podiatrists and patients prefer the soft orthotics.

5. Comfort. The plastic orthotics have a rigid edge that sometimes irritates the foot. Your foot spreads out as you run, and the edge can dig into your feet. This doesn't happen with soft orthotics.

Do I ever use plastic orthotics? I use a variation—Fiberglass supports within a soft orthotic. For instance, if you have heel spurs, I may use some extra support in that area—because that's the weight-bearing area of your foot, and that painful spot needs the weight taken off it.

Or, if a patient is overweight like me, he may need extra support. So I'll use a layer of Fiberglass in the weight-bearing area of the orthotics.

These are some reasons why I—and a lot of podiatrists—use the soft orthotics. If you've found a podiatrist who uses hard orthotics, I'm sure he has good reasons for it, and he'll be happy to discuss them with you.

7
Marathoning-

A Podiatrist's Eye-View

There are no accidental running injuries.

That's what runner/coach Tom Osler says. His statement may be a little exaggerated, but I think he's basically right. It's what I've been saying throughout this book: If you get an injury, you've probably been pushing yourself—either in training or in a race.

My experience with runners in the New York City Marathon confirms this point of view. After the latest New York City Marathon (1979), I got to thinking and comparing the marathons I've worked at over the last few years—in terms of how many runners needed treatment at the finish; how they ran the race; how well they prepared and trained for this grueling effort.

Marathons are an interesting laboratory for sports medicine. We get thousands of men and women going through an incredible test of fitness, strength and endurance. It's a great place for podiatrists—and runners—to learn about what causes injuries and what keeps runners healthy.

Actually, I never get to see the New York City Marathon. I only see the bruised and blistered remains of it—the aching runners who limp in, or are carried in to our little M.A.S.H. Unit at the finish line in Central Park.

I really enjoy working at the marathon. And, judging by the growing numbers of medical volunteers every year, I'd say a lot of people enjoy it. This year, we had about 130 volunteers. Most were podiatrists or podiatry students, and we're getting more and more physicians and nurses and some very hard-working chiropractors, therapists and medical masseurs. Our medical group at the finish line is the happiest field hospital you can imagine—tents and cots and blankets spread out under the trees, vats of E.R.G. and Gookinade and cases of Perrier for the thirsty warriors, and the Red Cross contribution—the world famous doughnuts and coffee.

First, there's the Lower Extremity Treatment Unit spread out over a large lawn. Then, up on a little hill, there are ambulances and mobile oxygen units for medical emergencies. Here you can see several runners lying on cots, receiving intravenous feedings of normal saline solution. According to Dr. Ed Colt, an endocrinologist who works year-round with the Road Runners Club, most runners treated here are suffering from heat exhaustion and leg cramps—which is one of the symptoms of heat exhaustion.

Down in the Lower Extremity area, I'd have to say the most common injury we see is blisters. Now and then a runner will arrive with something serious, like a sprained ankle. And, all day long, the medical masseurs are working on people with sore, cramped muscles. Dr. Mac Goldstein, a chiropractor, was there and I noticed he often put ice packs on cramped muscles before working on the runner. Mac explained that this anesthetizes the painful muscles and helps bring down the inflammation. It's also very soothing to the suffering athlete. Once the runner is feeling less pain, the chiropractor or therapist can work more effectively. Mac is a consultant to several college track teams, so I was glad to pick up this tip from someone who's so experienced with treating post-race problems.

Actually, we don't see all the "patients" at the finish line. This year, there were first aid stations along the whole route of the race. This innovation came from the organizers of the marathon's medical service—Dr. Louis Galli and Dr. Josef Geldwert, two very able podiatrists. So we have one first aid unit at the start of the race, one at the end, and sixteen more units all along the route—staffed by podiatrists, students and physicians and nurses from nearby hospitals. The New York City Marathon goes through the five boroughs of the city— so the local hospitals contributed volunteers.

The station at the start of the race will be expanded next year. The "patients" there are often runners who were afraid to go to a podiatrist before the marathon—because they might be told not to run.

What happens is, a runner has been working for months, all through the heat of the summer, preparing for this big race in the fall. Now, in the last week or so before the big event, he gets some aches or pains. But he grits his teeth and prays that the pain will just go away. The desire to run the marathon overcomes his common sense and he shows up, that cool October morning, wondering how he's going to get through the race and if it's really okay for him to run. Then he sees that there are some podiatrists on hand—so he rushes over for reassurance or some strapping or a pat on the head.

Basically, the volunteer medical unit is not meant to be a hospital that will treat any injury. And runners shouldn't think that it's all right to run in any condition, because there'll be doctors handy. We're simply there to give first aid and have ambulances available to send people to the hospital if necessary.

As runners check in for first aid all along the route—or at the finish line—podiatry students are there to get a few vital statistics. The point is to learn as much from this marathoning experience as possible. Information taken includes the runner's age, previous marathon experience, weekly training schedule, previous history of injury and what brand and model of shoe he's wearing. These statistics might answer several interesting questions. For instance—is there really a "wall"? Do more runners show up for treatment at the twenty-mile mark than at any other spot? Is there anything about shoe design that can be correlated with injuries? How much does your age and sex and amount of training affect your chances of being injured? These are some of the questions we're all trying to answer, as we meet and treat and talk with hundreds of marathoners each year.

I see a lot of my regular patients at the marathon, and find out how they've fared. One of these is my friend Dick Traum, a man who runs the marathon even though one of his legs is artificial. Dick was hit by a car in a gas station some years ago, and his leg was amputated eight inches above the knee. Dick was a college student at that time, and he was involved in collegiate wrestling. Part of his training for that sport was road work to build endurance. Now Dick says he runs to keep in shape, but he just wouldn't do it, unless he had a goal. So he does about four races a year.

Dick first came to me for runner's knee. His condition improved when he started wearing an orthotic device and doing exercises for the quadriceps. But runner's knee was not his only problem—he also has some arthritis in the knee. This means he can't run as many miles per week as he'd like. So, to keep up his endurance and his aerobic capacity, he pedals as much as a hundred miles a week on his bike. This keeps his leg muscles strong, without putting strain on the knee.

Dick says he doesn't really race the marathon—he navigates it. It takes him about eight hours to finish. In order to avoid the crush of runners, he starts at five in the morning—five hours before the official starting time—so he arrives at the finish with the three-hour marathoners. Dick treasures pictures of himself being passed by Bill Rodgers in the last few miles of the race.

I didn't see Dick at the end of this year's marathon. He had a few blisters, but he's an old-time runner, so he takes care of them himself. In fact, we saw fewer of *any* runners in the injury section this year. There were simply fewer injuries, even though there were more people running, and it was a hotter day than we had for the previous year's marathon. The statistics aren't all together yet, but I'd say about 300 people came in at the finish line for treatment. Only a small percentage of these needed intravenous feeding or other emergency treatment. Dr. Colt estimates that ten to twenty people were sent to the hospital with heat exhaustion—fewer than last year.

My theory is that runners are getting better trained and better educated. Runners are like sponges, they soak up every bit of information they can get—on vitamin C and shoes and exercises and different ways of doing intervals. All year long, they're learning and experimenting with their running. Then they show up at the marathon with a lot more training and understanding.

This year's runners also had more specific experience in running a marathon. In 1978, 39 percent of the men had never run a marathon before and 61 percent of the women. In 1979, roughly 25 percent of the men were first-timers and 50 percent of the women. So they knew how to train and how to run the course—and they got fewer injuries.

Also, they ran slower—and that may be another reason why they got fewer injuries. Allan Steinfeld, coordinator of the marathon, looked into his statistics and told me that the peak finishing time was later this year by about a half hour. For both 1978 and 1979, the peak time is between three and a half and four hours. But, in 1979, fewer people made it at three and a half; a lot more crossed under the finish banner at four hours. At 3:30 P.M., approximately 105 people per minute were crossing the finish. At 4 P.M., about 150 people were finishing every minute. And these were experienced runners who were probably capable of going a bit faster, if they wanted to push.

What happened? Allan theorizes that this year's higher temperatures told people to run slower and not to push. So they finished later—but with fewer injuries. It's a good lesson for all of us.

Of course, the runners who did show up with injuries have learned their lesson too. They've had it with marathons. The most frequent remark I hear in our outdoor emergency room is, "Oh my God! I'll never run another marathon!" It gives me a feeling of nostalgia. Because the same people were there last year saying the exact same thing.

PART TWO

8

How to Read Your Future in Your Feet

Or, What Injuries Mother Nature Has Set
You Up For And How to Avoid Them

The best way to avoid a problem is to be prepared for it.
Running is a beautiful, healthy sport—but it does put demands on your body. After a number of miles, you've got to
expect some wear and tear, a little strain on some of your
parts.

Yes, you may get an injury if you run a large number of
miles. Does this mean that the critics are right? That runners
would be better off sitting home? I don't think so. Everything
in life is a trade-off. You can stay home and keep your feet
comfortable. Or you can go out and run and develop a foot
problem (which is probably correctable), and in exchange,
you get a healthier heart and lungs, better circulation, leaner
body, stronger muscles, a fresher complexion and a better
disposition.

So I say run. But be prepared. If you were setting out on
a long automobile trip, you'd check your car and look for
weaknesses. Now you're a runner, and you're right at the start
of a nice long trip. I'm hoping you've got a lot of miles ahead

of you—whether you're a beginner or an experienced runner. So take a minute to check your feet. If you know what kind of feet you have, you'll know what injuries to expect. Virtually all running injuries start in the feet. This includes hip and back pains, as well as foot pains, knee pains, pulled thigh muscles and fractures in the legs and feet. No one was born with perfect, injury-proof feet. Even feet that have functioned beautifully for thirty or forty years suddenly start giving you problems when they're subjected to miles of pounding on hard paved roads.

But don't be alarmed—there's hope. The way I see it, running injuries are something like karma. According to certain Buddhist teachings, your karma, your life problems, are all set up before you're born. But if you make the right moves and have the right attitude, you can avoid or minimize the evil. It's the same with running injuries. If you know what to look for, you can take care of many problems before they start. And if you do get an injury, you'll know how to keep it from becoming serious.

So right now, I want you to look at your feet and start learning what kind of injury you're genetically programmed for.

Your First Toe's Shorter Than Your Second Toe

Actually, it's not your first toe that's short—it's the metatarsal bone it's attached to. You've got Morton's Foot—like so many of the athletes I see. Morton's foot contributes to many different injuries. It's one of the causes of painful knees, pain in the ball of the foot, callus under the second toe, hip pain, back pain, you name it.

Basically, your first metatarsal bone is too short to carry its share of the load. This means the weight gets shifted around, and all sorts of problems can happen. What you have to do is look up your particular problems—painful knees, hips, or whatever you're feeling—and you'll learn how to redistribute the weight and get rid of the pain.

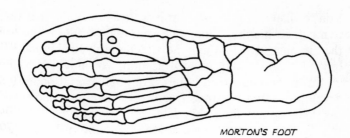

MORTON'S FOOT

Thin Feet with Prominent Bones

You may have perfectly constructed feet—arches the right height, well-proportioned bones, everything beautiful—but still have injuries because your feet don't have enough fat padding. Thin people aren't the only ones with thin feet. You could have fat padding all over your body and still have thin bony feet.

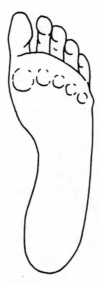

THIN FOOT WITH PROMINENT BONES

You're likely to get bone bruises, because your feet don't have much cushioning. One bone you might bruise is the head of the first metatarsal—the bone attached to your big toe.

If your feet are long as well as thin, you might get stress fractures in the metatarsal bones. Long metatarsal bones tend to develop tiny cracks (stress fractures) where the bone curves. Frank Shorter has long thin feet, and he has a lot of foot problems. But it doesn't seem to stop him, and it doesn't have to stop you either.

Read the chapter on "How to be Your Own Podiatrist" to learn about the various kinds of padding you can use to cushion your feet. Also, the section on Sesamoiditis will be helpful to you; and the section on pain on top of the foot, along the shaft of the bone in chapter 9. This section tells you how metatarsal stress fractures are treated.

Fallen Arches (Weak Foot)

You can see this problem better when you stand on your feet and put your weight on them. Notice how the ankles turn in and the weight falls toward the inside of the foot. (In technical terms, your foot pronates.)

Here's another test. Stand up and try to lay a pencil on the floor, running from your heel to your first metatarsal head. If your arches are normal, you can do it—because there's a straight line between those two points. But if you have fallen arches, the pencil will angle out.

This condition, which used to be called fallen arches, is now known as weak foot. It can lead to knee pain, lower back pain, Achilles pain (that's pain in the back of the lower leg, just above the ankle). You may get pain in the heel and arch (Plantar Fasciitis and Heel Spurs). You're subject to pain on the inner side of the lower leg—somewhere in the area where the large calf muscle meets the shin muscle. People with fallen arches get it all.

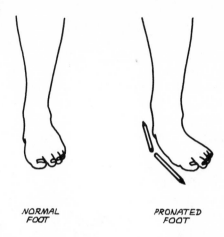

NORMAL
FOOT

PRONATED
FOOT

But don't worry—a lot of us weak-footed folks are out
there running and having a fine time. You just have to know
how to take care of your feet.

I was born with low arches, and I've developed fallen
arches over the years. I've observed over the years that Sem-
ites (Jews and Arabs) and Blacks are more likely to have low
arches than other people are. One of my patients asked me if
this was because we Jews have been wandering for so many
years. Another one of those interesting questions that I can't
answer.

In any case, your feet are going to demand a lot of attention. Read the section on Weak Foot and read the section on
each of your symptoms as it comes along.

Incidentally, you don't have to be born with low arches to
get fallen arches. People who are born with high or ordinary
arches have a good shot at it too.

High-Arched Foot

High arches can "fall" too—often sooner than low-arched
feet. Romance people—French, Italians, Spanish—are more

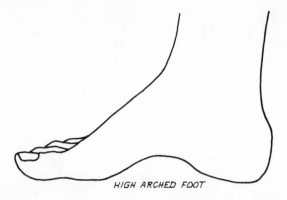

HIGH ARCHED FOOT

likely to have a high arched foot. Also, in my experience, I've found that many people with very high-arched feet tend to be thin, tense people.

If your high-arched foot starts collapsing, you too, develop the weak foot symptoms—so read the section on weak foot.

High arches are less flexible. So you may develop Impact Shock, Heel Bruise and Metatarsal Bruise. There are things you can do to treat these injuries, if you've got them. And there are ways to help prevent them. So read those sections and learn how to keep yourself running in comfort.

Extremely High-Arched Foot with Retracted Toes (Cavus Foot)

The cavus type of foot has a very high arch and high instep and the toes are a little retracted. Your foot can be good and solid—well-balanced, as far as weight distribution goes—but the high arch leads to a lot of troubles.

You can get pain on the bottom of the heel and arch (read plantar fasciitis; heel spurs in chapter 9). You may get pain and calluses on the bottom of the foot where the toes connect to the metatarsal bones (read pain and calluses on the ball of the foot). You can also get pain under the three middle toes, where they connect to the metatarsal bones (read anterior

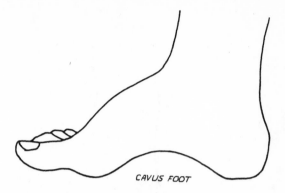

CAVUS FOOT

metatarsal bursitis). You're liable to get corns on the top of your toes. (Try slitting the tops of your running shoes to give your toes more room.) You may also get corns on the tips of the toes. Read the section on corns in chapter 9, to learn what to do—and what not to do—about corns.

Your cavus foot needs a lot of care, no question about it. But if you'll read about each symptom as it comes up, you can give your feet the intelligent care they need and keep them running comfortably.

Feet with Bunions

A bunion is an enlargement of the bone attached to your big toe. (A tailor's bunion is the same thing, only with the little toe.) If you have bunions, your big toe may be turned in toward the second toe, and tucked under or over the second toe. But people with straight first toes get bunions too.

I don't have to tell you that bunions can be painful. But what you should be aware of is that running can cause extra problems. Some doctors believe that the repeated pressure of running can cause bunions to enlarge even more. This may or may not be true. In any case, all the weight you put on the bunion by running can cause extra pain. (When you run, you come down with a force equal to three times your body

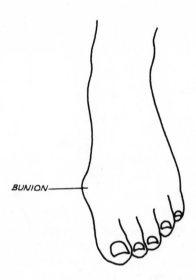

weight.)

The right running shoes are important for everyone, but especially for people with bunions. Badly fitting shoes can make your bunions even more painful. But you didn't get them from bad shoes or anything else. You were just born to have bunions. Or at least with a tendency to bunions. Read the section on How to Buy Shoes and the section on Bunions— and learn how to take care of them.

Short Bunchy Calf Muscles

This doesn't go with any particular type of foot. But you should be aware that your kind of leg is more susceptible to certain injuries—shin splints, Achilles tendonitis, pain in the back of the knee and tight hamstrings.

Basically, you need lots of stretching and lots of attention to your running habits. Read the chapter on Exercises to

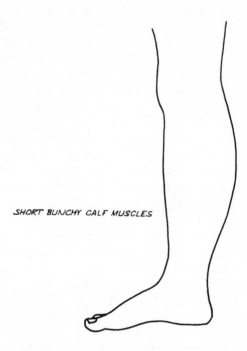

SHORT BUNCHY CALF MUSCLES

Prevent Injuries, and concentrate especially on the Wall Push-ups and Hamstring Stretches. And read the chapter on How to Run Right, and Hurt Less.

The Ideal Runner's Foot?

Nature has not yet published her plan for the perfect modern runner's foot—a foot that can run on concrete roads for the ever-increasing distances that today's runners love—and never get an injury. Since nature hasn't revealed her design, I'm not sticking my neck out either. I don't know what the perfect running foot would be. But a short, stubby, well-balanced foot —a wide foot with plenty of fat padding—would be an excellent piece of running equipment for city streets.

If you're running in the jungle, you could use a less firm and less perfectly balanced foot because running on uneven terrain requires a more flexible foot. And if one part of your foot doesn't fit well with the patch of earth you've landed on, then another part, another toe, *will* fit. Also, the jungle terrain is softer and doesn't give the body such a jolt with every step. So our ancestors' running was less demanding than our running.

But my tentative plans for the perfect modern runner's foot is a short, wide, pudgy foot. The fat padding protects you from bone bruises. The short bones are less likely to fracture. The width gives you a more stable base. The first toe is slightly longer than the second and third. This means that each toe and metatarsal bone will carry its proper amount of weight as you run. The arch isn't too high or too low. Either of these can lead to fallen arches. Come to think of it, medium arches have a good chance of falling too.

This ideal foot would have strong muscles on the bottom. And strong post-tibial muscles. (These are muscles that go from the inner side of the lower leg down to the arch. They help support the arch.) I'd also make the material on the bottom of the foot (the plantar fascia) strong and resilient —but not too resilient.

You see how easy it is to have a less-than-perfect runner's foot?

Ideally, this short fat foot should be connected to a leg with long, slender muscles. These are muscles that stay injury-free, while we less fortunate people with short, bunchy muscles get all sorts of stiffness and tightness in the lower leg.

Until the perfect foot comes along, my experience has shown me that we've all got an excellent chance at having some kind of injury. So learn what kind of foot nature gave you, and learn how to take care of it.

9
Runners' Injuries and How to Treat Them Yourself

One Leg Shorter than the Other

(Don't say no—it's the first thing you should check.)

No matter what your injury, there's a chance that it's aggravated by short-leg.

Think of a line running from the tips of your toes along your arch, then up the back of your leg and your spine. If one of your legs is shorter than the other, it can cause (or aggravate) a pain or strain anywhere along that line.

The pain can come on the shorter side or the longer side. A lot of us have one leg shorter than the other and don't even know it. It doesn't really matter, if it isn't causing you any pain. Before you started running, you may have been perfectly comfortable with one leg ¼-inch shorter. Now you start running and with every running step, you come down with three times your body weight. If you weigh a hundred fifty pounds, you're socking four hundred and fifty pounds onto a leg that's a bit unbalanced anyway because it's shorter than the other.

To think of it another way—it's as if one leg were ¾-inch shorter, instead of ¼-inch.

So the first step for many injuries is to check your leg length. Do this if you've got arch pains, knee pains, hip or back pains, shin pains.

How to Compare Your Leg Lengths   There are two ways you should compare your leg lengths: Compare the distance from the knees to the floor; and the distance from the hipbone to the floor. In this second step, you're actually checking to see whether your hips are level. If they're not, we say you have "pelvic tilt."

To check the lengths of your lower legs (from knee to floor), get a carpenter's level and check your floor to find a place where the floor is level. Now put a straight-backed chair there. Check to be sure the chair is level.

Take off your shoes and socks. Sit with your back against the back of the chair. Put the carpenter's level on your knees and see if the bubble is in the middle. If not, you've got one short leg.

To see if your hips are level, you need a full-length mirror, a piece of string and a felt-tipped pen. Just stand in front of the mirror naked and mark each hip bone with a dot—the bone that sticks out farthest.

Now hold the string from one dot to the other, and you can see if it's level.

Next, check your hips from the rear. Very often, an imbalance shows up in the rear when it doesn't show up in front.

You'll need a helper for this. First, he takes a felt-tipped pen and puts a mark in the dimple above each buttock. Second, he draws a line across the top of your hipbone. To find where to mark, he just feels for the outline of your hipbone, and draws a line on the bone.

Now he compares: Are the two hipbone lines level? Are the dots in the dimples level? He can decide just by looking, or by using the carpenter's level.

If your hips are not level, you either have one short leg or

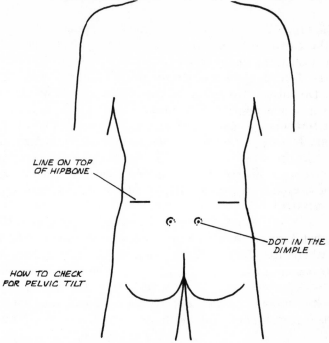

LINE ON TOP
OF HIPBONE

DOT IN THE
DIMPLE

HOW TO CHECK
FOR PELVIC TILT

there's some other reason why one hip is higher than the
other. It could be that your spine curves to one side. But
whatever the reason—if your hips are uneven you do have
one short leg, in effect. It may be that your hip is pulling
your leg up and making it short.

So you have to treat yourself for one short-leg—and that
means simply putting a heel pad in one shoe.

Sponge rubber makes a good heel pad. If your leg is
¼-inch short, use padding slightly thinner than a ¼-inch.
Your sponge rubber should be ³⁄₁₆-inch thick. If your leg is
½-inch short, use sponge rubber ⅜-inch thick. If your leg
is ¾-inch short, use padding slightly thinner than three-
quarters of an inch.

If your discrepancy is greater than ¾-inch, see a podiatrist.
He'll probably give you a little padding under the sole, as well
as under the heel. You can't just stick padding under your
heel, if you have too great a difference in your leg lengths.

I tell my patients to use Victex makeup sponges for heel pads. You can buy them in Woolworth's. Or you can buy virtually the same thing, under the name "Jogheel."

Wear your heel pad in your running shoes and your daytime shoes. And then follow the other recommended treatment for your symptom. For instance, if you have pain in the arch, read the section on weak foot, and see if that's your problem. If it is, you have to treat yourself for weak foot, as well as for short-leg.

Of course, you never correct a leg-length discrepancy unless it's causing you trouble. If your legs and back are absolutely pain-free and you happen to find out you have one short leg, don't worry about it. Apparently your body has learned to function with one short leg, and we don't want to upset a balance that's working well for you.

But, if you do have pain in the legs or spine, and you find you have short-leg, use the heel pad. If it doesn't seem to help—say in about a week—take the heel pad out. If the heel pad doesn't help, it could hurt.

First Toe Shorter than Second

(Morton's Foot)

Actually, it's not your first toe that's short. It's the first metatarsal bone it's attached to. If you have Morton's foot, you're

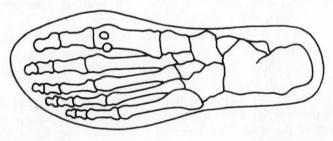

MORTON'S FOOT

in good company. A lot of the top athletes I see in my office have this kind of foot. Why do I see so many of them? Because Morton's foot causes all sorts of problems.

Here's why. When you run, you're supposed to push off on the first and second toe. Actually, between the first and second metatarsals. But a short first metatarsal can't quite carry its share of the weight; so the weight is tilted toward the inside of the foot.

This twist is sent right up the leg and spine—so it can cause knee problems, hip problems, all kinds of problems. It can cause a callus under the second toe, because the first toe is not carrying its share of weight. Your second metatarsal bone will become thicker.

Because so many different injuries can develop from a Morton's foot, we won't try to explain them all here. Just look up each problem under its symptom: painful knees, painful ball of the foot, callus under the second toe, hip pain, back pain.

Stiff Big Toe

Your big toe feels rigid or almost rigid. It's so painful, you've been cutting down on your mileage. But your toe is still painful.

If you came into my office, the first thing I'd do is take hold of your toe and move it up and down. Try it. Do you feel a grating, sandpapery feeling? If so, you may have arthritis and calcium deposits in the joint between the toe and the metatarsal.

But whether you do or not, the answer is to lift the toe up a bit from the ground so it's not getting bumped and pounded every time you run.

Your shoemaker can put a strip of Neoprene, hard rubber, on the sole of your shoe—right behind the ball of the foot. This goes on the outside of the shoe, not on the insole. Tell him to take hard rubber, about ⅛-inch thick. Cut it 1¼-inches

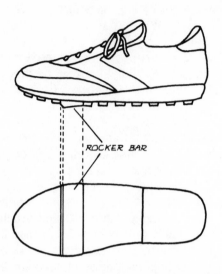

ROCKER BAR

wide and long enough to go across the entire width of the shoe—right behind the widest part of the shoe. (In a shoe that fits properly, the ball of the foot comes at the widest part of the shoe.) He should taper the front and back edges of the strip, so it's not a big bump.

The strip of rubber should come just behind the metatarsal heads. The metatarsals are the bones your toes are attached to.

Now, with this addition to your shoe, your foot rocks right over the strip of rubber when you run. You've taken some of the impact off the ball of the foot and the big toe.

Pain under First Metatarsal Head, Bone Attached to Big Toe

(Sesamoiditis)

You may have increased your mileage lately, or maybe you're doing hill work or speed work—activities where you're run-

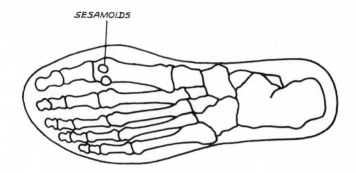

SESAMOIDS

ning on the ball of the foot.

Now, under the head of the first metatarsal bone, you have two or maybe three or four tiny bones called sesamoids. These tiny pealike bones are found at various places in the body. They're remains from our evolutionary past. One thing they do for a runner is to protect the first metatarsal head—because they get hurt before it does.

To see if you've bruised these bones, feel the bottom of your foot with your fingers. Press gently on the first metatarsal head. Look for swelling. You may or may not find any. Now press hard on the first metatarsal head with your thumb —from the bottom of the foot upward. If you feel an excruciating pain, that's it—you've either bruised or broken your sesamoids, and it doesn't matter which. The treatment is the same.

The first step is to ice them. Put some ice cubes in a plastic bag. Twist the bag closed. Then put the bag into a basin, and put your foot on it. Or, use one of the commercial ice bags sold in running stores.

Put your foot on ice for ten minutes, then take it off ten minutes, then repeat. Do this three or four times a day.

Now, second step—the long term treatment—is to correct the conditions that bruised or broke your bones in the first place.

What's happened is, running and pounding on the ball of the foot has put too much pressure on it. You may have been running on hard pavement. Or maybe you've been doing a lot of hill work or sprinting. When you do, you're continually landing on the ball of the foot. Or maybe you just have a habit of running on the balls of the feet. You've got to correct that.

A little running on the ball of the foot, when you're sprinting for a short distance, that's okay. But if you're running for miles on the ball of the foot, you're asking for trouble.

Your heel should hit the ground first. Then the middle of the foot. Then you take off from the ball of the foot—use it as a spring, not a landing platform.

Or maybe you haven't done anything wrong in your running—maybe you've just got a bony foot. The head of the first metatarsal sticks out, and an awful lot of weight is going on that one spot.

Whatever the reason for your problem—part of the cure is to give yourself a bigger platform to take off from. The first metatarsal head is just one little knob; so pad around it and spread the impact.

I would get a piece of felt pad, about ¼-inch thick—say 3-by-2 inches in size—and cut a sort of U in it, to fit around the first metatarsal head. Don't put padding over the metatarsal head—that's got too much pressure on it already.

The way to find the right spot is, just press with your thumb until you feel that excruciating pain, and then put your pad behind that. When I say "behind," I mean in the direction of the heel. I would bevel the edges of the pad that go toward the arch—taper off the edges—so you're not standing on a lump.

For your pad you can use felt or foam rubber or Dr. Scholl's Heel Pads. These are made of foam rubber covered with plastic, so they stay neater. When you put tape on and then pull it off, the plastic doesn't pull apart the way foam rubber does. When the plastic gets too sticky, you can either buy new pads or clean off the stickiness with nail polish remover. You buy all these in any drug store.

Whatever material you use for padding, hold it over the

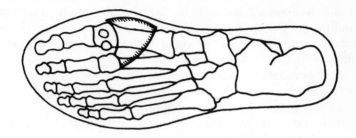

PADDING FOR SESAMOIDITIS

first metatarsal head. Now feel with your fingers and draw the outline of the bone. Then cut out the U-shape to go behind the bone. Don't pad in front of the bone (under the toes).

You can tell your padding is right when you stand and walk on it. You get a great feeling of comfort. You've got a more solid foundation. And the pressure is off that painful bone. If one pad doesn't feel thick enough, use two. You can glue or tape them together.

Whichever kind of padding you use, tape it on with the clear tape that's sold on the foot care stand. Or ordinary adhesive tape. Or use elasticized tape (Elastoplast—your druggist can order it for you if he doesn't carry it).

Wear this padding in your running shoes and in your daytime shoes. Women should stick to flat shoes until the pain is gone. You may always have to wear these pads for your running or you'll bruise your sesamoids all over again. So, once you've figured out the right position for your pads, try gluing them inside your running shoes.

You should be able to start running right away, and the pain should be completely gone in about two weeks. If it isn't, the problem is with the way your foot balances. Your foot may be putting too much weight on the first metatarsal head. It has to do with the length of the bones and the strength of the arches.

In that case, you need a corrective support for your whole

foot—an orthotic device that you wear inside your shoes. It gives your foot the strength it's lacking in certain places, so you'll stop shifting too much weight over to the ball of the foot. Your podiatrist can design a custom-made orthotic from a mold of your foot.

My co-author, Barbara Burr, and I have a special affection for sesamoiditis, because that's what brought us together.

Barbara had been running happily with no foot problems until she reached the point of running about four miles a day on a regular basis. Then she noticed the pain in her first metatarsal head and in the big toe. (Barbara has arthritis in the big toe which only flares up when the sesamoid bones are bruised.)

Like many runners, she owned a lot of running books and has a lot of running friends to consult. No book—and no other runner—came up with the answer for her mysterious aching foot. So she checked with Dr. Sheehan, who sent her to me.

I found that her foot was perfectly balanced. Her only problem was that she has bony feet without much fat padding. So the first metatarsal head sticks out sharply and bruises easily.

I corrected this with an orthotic that puts padding around the first metatarsal head and has a hollow for the bone to sit in. Barbara wears these in her running shoes and all her low-heeled shoes. For higher-heeled shoes, she sometimes tapes pads onto her foot—pads she makes herself.

Once her foot problem was solved, Barbara decided the world needed a book telling runners exactly how to care for their feet. So here it is.

Big Toe Bunions

A bunion is that enlarged bone connecting to the big toe that sticks out at the side. (The head of the first metatarsal bone is enlarged.)

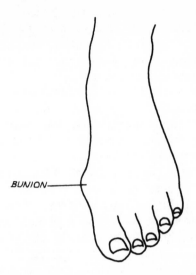

BUNION

A tendency to bunions is something that you inherited. But the size of the bunion increases—and the irritation increases—if you put too much weight and shoe pressure on it.

Why are you putting too much weight on your bunion? Very often, your big toe is angled in—it tucks under or over your second toe. This causes a weight-distribution problem. A lot of your weight drops down onto that first metatarsal head, so the bone grows bigger to support the load.

Many people think of bone as being a very hard, rigid material. Actually, it's fairly adaptable. It will get bigger in response to its surroundings—even when we're adults.

If you tied a tight bandage around your forearm, in time the bone would become narrower under the bandage, and you'd have an indentation around your arm.

With a bunion, your foot is putting extra weight on the first metatarsal head—so the bone grows bigger to handle the extra weight. But this process is not reversible. You can't shrink a bunion. You can only make it more comfortable. Or you can trim it down, surgically.

The pressure of the weight might also give you a callus

under the second metatarsal head (the bone connected to the second toe). Or you might get a corn on top of the second toe. That happens when the big toe is bent in toward the second toe. Your second toe is then crowded and pushed upward, so it rubs against your shoe.

To make your bunion more comfortable, you can buy a bunion pad. It covers the whole area, but the material that goes over the bunion is thinner. You don't want to put thick padding over the bunion, because that will cause more pressure when you put your shoe on.

Or make yourself a bunion bagel. Take a piece of foam rubber and hold it over the bunion. Now take a pencil and draw the shape of the bunion on the pad. Then cut out the shape of the bunion, so when you tape the bagel on, your bunion sticks out through the hole. If one pad isn't thick enough to give relief, glue two pads together. Of course, you'll have to be sure your shoe is wide enough to take this extra padding.

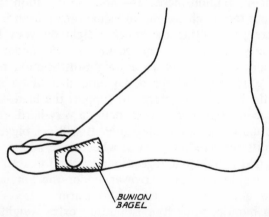

BUNION
BAGEL

If you have a bunion, and your big toe is angled in, the joint can become irritated. You can protect the joint by putting a latex jacket over the toe. This jacket covers the outside of the bunion to protect the joint. It leaves the tip of the toe uncovered.

I'll sometimes prescribe a custom-made latex jacket to protect a bunion. I make a mold of the toe and the metatarsal
head, and that's used to make a latex jacket. The jacket is
made with space for the bunion and any corn you may have.
It's a highly sophisticated corn pad that protects the whole
area and gives you a lot of comfort.

Or sometimes I'll make an orthotic device—a special lining
for the shoe—that keeps pressure off the bunion. I explained
that your bunion grows and becomes irritated when you put
too much weight on it. So if you put some padding under
your arch, the arch will take more weight, or it will redistribute the weight. Now there's less pressure on the bunion.

Try a commercial arch support. That can shift the weight
load and may give you a lot of relief.

Now, check and be sure you've done these three things:

1. You've stopped wearing shoes that are too tight. You've
stopped wearing extremely high-heeled shoes. (They throw
too much weight forward onto the bunion and force your
bunion into the narrower part of the shoe.)

2. You've tried wearing a bunion bagel or latex jacket or
other cushioning.

3. You've tried wearing a commercial arch support.

If you're still having trouble with your bunions, you'd better see a sports-oriented podiatrist. You need a podiatrist who
works with the mechanics of the body in motion, because
your problem is probably caused by the way your weight
moves along your foot as you walk and run. He may find that
your foot is imbalanced in some way, and he can make an
orthotic device to balance you out.

If you don't know a good podiatrist, read the section in
chapter 5 on "How to Choose a Podiatrist If You Need One."

One of my patients—Barbara Backer—came to me with
very painful bunions. She had always had bunions, but they
never bothered her until she got up to four or five miles of

running per day and was doing a lot of hill work and speed work.

In analyzing Barbara's running style, we found that she had been taking off from her bunions. When you run, you should take off from an area between the first and second metatarsals. But Barbara's weight was rolling in, onto the bunion.

I took some Plastizote, a fairly soft, cushiony material, and made pads that fit right under her arches. I glued these into her running shoes. This gave her a more solid foundation, and her weight doesn't roll onto the bunion anymore.

Barbara now runs sixty miles a week, and her bunions are no problem.

Another way to relieve pressure on your bunion is to make a slit in your running shoes. Don't make a big hole that would let the bunion stick out entirely. If you do, your bunion will start scraping the ground as you run. That's not too comfortable.

What about surgery for bunions?

If your big toe angles in under the second toe, it is possible to straighten it out through surgery and trim down the bunion. But this would keep you out of running from six-to-ten weeks. And you're leaving yourself open to some other complication, like rigidity of the joint.

If your bunion is chronically painful and you can't live with it, you may have to resort to surgery. But if you can keep it comfortable with a little pad in the shoe, that's a lot better.

Now that you've learned to take pressure off the bunion, don't put the pressure back on with tight shoes. The key with painful bunions is to get shoes with plenty of space over the ball of the foot. That solves half the problem. Some women wear strap shoes winter and summer to let the bunion stick out. That makes sense, if your feet don't get too cold.

Some doctors think running makes bunions worse by putting extra pressure on them. I'm not so sure about that. I am sure that tight shoes make them worse, but tight shoes alone will not create bunions. If you weren't born to have bunions, you just won't have them.

If you look back in your family history, you'll find your mother had bunions or your grandmother had them. Now they're yours; so take good care of them.

Small Toe Bunions

You can also get a bunion on the bone connecting to your little toe. This is called a tailor's bunion because tailors used to sit cross-legged and put pressure on the outside of the foot, and that would cause a bunion. So there's an exception to what I just said—if you sit cross-legged eight hours a day you can get a bunion without any help from your genes.

If you have a tailor's bunion, treat it as you would a big-toe bunion. Protect it with a bunion bagel and keep your shoes wide enough, or make a slit in your running shoes to give the bunion space.

Pain in Big Toe Tendon, Connection of Toe to Foot

Even if you have a perfectly designed foot—no bunions, toes all the proper lengths and so on—you may feel pain where the big toe connects to the metatarsal bone. The tendon that lifts the big toe may be prominent and it gets irritated if you wear the wrong shoes.

Where the shoe bends, it's hitting the tendon, and you may get a corn, a sore or an ulceration. This is a shoe problem, not a foot problem. Just figure out which of your shoes is causing the pain and get rid of them. And pay extra attention to how the shoes hit that tendon whenever you buy new ones.

Toes that Can't Straighten Out

(Hammer Toes)

Take your index finger and bend it so the joint sticks up. That's how a hammer toe looks, and generally you can't straighten it out. Some hammer toes can straighten out, but they prefer to stay bent. Any toe except the big toe could be a hammer toe.

Hammer toes are caused by shoes that are too short. The shoe forces the toe back, so the tendon on top of the toe eventually shortens. And the top of the toe really hurts when you run.

A tendon is a cord that's somewhat elastic, but not very. The tendon on top of your toe may have become so short over a long period of time that it can't stretch out again.

Hammer toes don't hurt except you often get a corn on the top. And runners with hammer toes sometimes get a corn right on the tip of the toe.

Just be sure your shoes are loose enough to keep the pressure off the toes. If you can't get running shoes that are loose enough over the toe, cut a slit in the top of the shoes.

If you already have a corn, put an aperture pad on it—a doughnut pad—or wrap lamb's wool all around the toe. I really prefer lamb's wool to a doughnut. If you wear a doughnut on a regular basis, the area all around the corn gets pressed down. So, in effect, the corn is sticking up even higher.

Wrap the lamb's wool around your whole toe three or four times, then twist and press the ends so they blend in together. Lamb's wool is waterproof, so you can leave it on when you shower. It lasts three or four days.

You can buy lamb's wool on the foot care stand in your drugstore. Get the kind that's silky, sort of like angel hair. This is different from the lamb's wool that ballet dancers use. They use uncarded lamb's wool—it's nubby, like steel wool.

If you have a corn on the front of a hammer toe, use the

lamb's wool. And also put some padding under the toe.

Your bent toes have created a big empty arch underneath. Put padding in that arch so your toes are lifted up. Then the front of your toes won't slam into the bottom of the shoe when you run. This relieves the pressure on the corn.

For padding, you can buy a crest pad in the drugstore. Another good padding is one of the cotton sticks your dentist uses. See if he'll give you some.

Or, make your own padding "sticks." Take moleskin, three-inches wide. Roll up a tube. Use enough moleskin to make the tube ¼-inch in diameter. Now wrap gauze around it to hold it together.

Cut the tube so it's long enough to fit under the three middle toes. Put the tube under the crest of the toes and wrap tape around the three toes, including the padding. Now when you run, you're not hitting the tips of the toes. Your weight is landing on the bottom surface of the toes, where it's supposed to be.

CREST PAD

Pain/Calluses on Ball of Foot

(Prominent metatarsals; bruised and inflamed metatarsals)

Feel the bottom of your foot, and find your metatarsal arch—right where the toes connect to the heads of the metatarsals. As you press along there, starting at the first metatarsal and moving along to the second and third, you should feel an arch. The second, third and fourth metatarsal heads should be higher. Then the arch goes down again, as you get to the fifth metatarsal head.

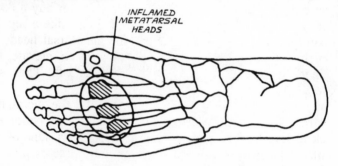

If you don't feel an arch there—and you feel calluses on the bones—you've got a prominent metatarsal arch.

A prominent metatarsal arch can give you bruised bones. Inflammation. Calluses and even corns on the bottom of the foot.

With a prominent metatarsal arch, your second, third or fourth metatarsals are lower than they should be. So let's lift them up. Take a piece of felt or sponge rubber ¼-inch thick, and put it right behind the heads of those metatarsal bones.

How do you know where to put the padding? Bend your toes back and feel the painful area where the toes connect to the metatarsals. Press and find the spot that really hurts. Good, that's the metatarsal head. A callused, bruised or inflamed metatarsal head is going to hurt if you press on it.

You may have one or two or three metatarsals causing trouble. Once you've found the guilty parties, tape your

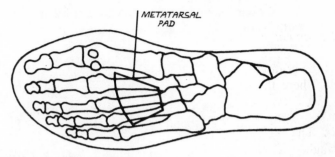

METATARSAL
PAD

padding just behind them.

You can also buy metatarsal pads. Or you can buy a commercial arch with metatarsal pads in it. It looks like a regular arch support, but it's padded behind the metatarsal heads.

Whichever padding you use, the idea is to elevate the prominent metatarsal and take the pressure off. That will relieve the pain.

You can also do some exercises that make the metatarsal arch strong and more flexible. That may help your condition.

Pick up towels with your toes. Pick up pencils. One of my patients, ballerina Melissa Hayden, has her students pick up marbles with their toes. Then she has them pick up a marble with one toe at a time.

Also, when picking up a towel with the toes—Melissa tells her students to press on the toes as you draw them up. Don't jerk them up. Then as you flatten them out, press them down again. Always work with a slow, steady motion.

These exercises tighten up the arch and also stretch the tendons on top—the ones that help lift the toes. If you do these exercises too long, you'll get cramps in the long arch. But that's just a signal to stop and rest.

Pain under Three Lesser Toes

(Anterior metatarsal bursitis)

This is not an injury to the toes. It's the metatarsal bones that are hurt—the bones connecting to the toes. Feel in between the toe and the metatarsal head. Press with your fingers, and you'll feel pain.

What's happened is you're coming down too hard on that area. So your body builds up a little protective cushion there —a bursa. Now, when you continue to run and put more pressure on the same area, the bursal sac gets irritated. It's swollen and painful. (You won't feel the sac with your fingers —just pain.)

The cure is to put padding behind the heads of the metatarsals. This puts some cushioning around the metatarsal heads, so you won't be slamming down on them so hard.

Where should you put the cushioning? Bend your toes back and press till you find the spots that hurt. Now tape the padding behind those spots. (Behind, meaning in the direction of the heel.)

Some good pads to use are commercial metatarsal pads. Or take a piece of sponge rubber, ¼-inch thick. Cut out a piece two- or three-inches long—long enough to go behind the painful metatarsal heads. Make the pad about two inches deep. Then tape the padding on.

Another way to take pressure off the metatarsal heads is to lower your heels. If you're a woman, stop wearing high heels until the pain clears up.

It also helps to put padding in *front* of the painful area. You can do this with a crest pad which you buy in the drugstore. It puts padding under the crest of your toes.

Another way to put padding under the crest of the toes is to get some cotton sticks from your dentist and put them under the three middle toes. Wrap tape around the three toes, including the cotton stick.

If you can't get these dental sticks, make a "stick" with moleskin. Get moleskin three-inches wide. Roll it until you make a stick that's a ¼-inch in diameter.

Doctors will often use injection therapy—steroids or Xylocaine or Novocaine—to bring down the inflammation in bruised metatarsals. I prefer padding, because any drug may have some side effects.

Now, why did you get this bursitis? Why are you putting too much weight on that area of your foot?

Most likely there's some imbalance in your foot—so the weight isn't distributed properly. Too much weight is falling on the ball of your foot. If the pain doesn't clear up in a few weeks with your own padding, go to a sports-oriented podiatrist. He may decide to give you an orthotic, made from a mold of your foot, that will redistribute the weight. Or he can teach you how to pad your own shoes.

Exercising can help too. Pick up towels with your toes. Pick up pencils. These same exercises strengthen the long arch of your foot too, so your whole foundation is stronger and steadier. And that's something every runner wants.

Burning Sensation between Bases of Toes

(Neuromas)

You'll feel this burning sensation between the metatarsal heads and reaching out into the toes. It usually happens between the third and fourth metatarsal heads. But it can occur in the others.

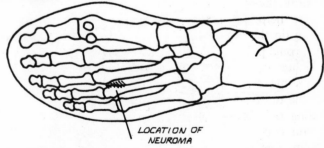

LOCATION OF
NEUROMA

Some people describe this sensation as shooting pains or electric tingling pains. But I usually hear people say they've got a burning sensation reaching out through the third and fourth toes. It's an excruciating pain and you can't bear weight on it.

You've got a neuroma—a bundle of nerve endings whose covering or sheath has become inflamed and irritated. Very often it happens in a loose foot, a foot that's got too much movement between the metatarsals.

There's no swelling. You can't feel any bumps. You can't even see neuromas on an X ray. You know you've probably got a neuroma by the symptoms—shooting, burning pains or a numb sensation. Runners often say they had to stop running and take off their shoe to massage the foot. But the pain can come on at odd times, even when you're not running or walking.

The first thing you should do is give it ice treatment. Put some ice cubes in a plastic bag and twist the bag closed. Or, if you've got one of those ice bags they sell in running stores, use that.

Put this ice bag in a basin, and put your foot on it. Leave your foot on ice ten minutes, then take it off ten minutes. Repeat four or five times. This will bring down some of the inflammation.

Next, let's get the pressure off those nerve bundles. Put some padding right behind the spot where the metatarsal heads connect to the toes—whichever toes are hurting.

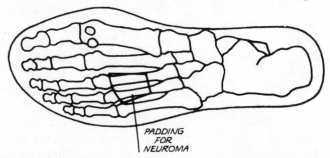

PADDING
FOR
NEUROMA

To find the right spot, bend your toes back and press on the bottom of your foot until you find the most painful spot. Put the padding behind that—in the direction of the heel.

Use ¼-inch thick padding—surgical felt or foam rubber.

Or, you can buy metatarsal pads. They're good.

Wear this padding and keep using your ice treatments two or three times a day for a couple of weeks and the pain should be relieved.

You'll probably have to keep wearing those pads all your life whenever you run, because the bones themselves are putting pressure on the neuroma and causing pain. So, why not glue the pads into your running shoes to save time. Even though the nerve bundles will always be there, they shouldn't hurt as long as you wear the padding—because there's no pressure on them.

Also, be sure that your shoes are wide enough. The tighter your shoes, the more pressure on those nerves. Another good idea is to lower your heels and take some weight off the ball of the foot. If you're a woman, try wearing lower heels.

To repeat: Your home treatment is icing and padding and proper shoes. If you've tried these for two or three weeks and you're still in pain, you'd better get professional help. In my office, the first thing I do for neuromas is make a foot support with special padding that lifts and separates the bones around the neuroma. That works most of the time.

Or your doctor might use injection therapy—steroids or maybe some vitamin B_{12} mixed with Xylocaine or Novocaine. Steroids reduce the inflammation and may even cause the nerve endings to become less sensitive.

Very often, you can solve the problem with one of these approaches. If none of these works, I would then remove the neuroma surgically, and that definitely works. It's one of the few conditions in running where we might have to resort to surgery.

This operation is not very disabling because we're just removing soft tissue, not bone, and you can stand on your feet the first day after the operation. In a couple of weeks you're out running again.

Pain on Top of Foot, Along Bone Shaft
(Could be a stress fracture of a metatarsal bone)

The metatarsals—those long thin bones that attach to your toes—can be bruised or broken under the stress of running. Soldiers and back packers do the same kind of damage when they walk for miles carrying heavy packs.

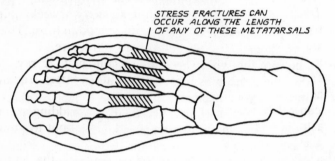

STRESS FRACTURES CAN OCCUR ALONG THE LENGTH OF ANY OF THESE METATARSALS

Stress fractures are insidious. You don't know when they're happening because there's no sudden snap. Actually, it isn't one fracture. It's many micro-fractures that occur somewhere along the shaft of the bone—usually where it bends a little.

What are the signals of stress fracture?

When you run you feel pain in a specific metatarsal. You may feel pain when you walk. There may even be a little area of redness or swelling on top of the foot. If you press right at that point, the pain will really be excruciating. Press along the shaft of the bone toward the outside and then toward the inside. You'll get a real stabbing pain.

This pain is a pretty good indication that you've got a stress fracture. But the doctor will have to x-ray to corroborate.

A stress fracture is not something you should try to treat yourself. Get an appointment as quickly as possible with a podiatrist or orthopedic surgeon. Of course, stop running. Immobilize the foot as much as possible.

Women should not wear high heels. Actually, the best thing to wear is wooden clogs to keep any motion from occurring at the metatarsal area. With a clog, you lift your foot and plant it down flat. You don't bend the foot at all.

Men don't usually have clogs so the doctor may give you a wooden shoe called a Reese boot.

The doctor will probably examine your foot by feeling along the metatarsal bone in the way I described above. Then he'll take an X ray. The X ray may not show any signs of stress fractures—especially if it's soon after the injury. A stress fracture doesn't show up until about two weeks later, when some scar tissue (bone callus) has started to form. That's how you know for sure that you've had a fracture.

Even though nothing shows up on the first X ray, the doctor's clinical judgment may tell him it's a stress fracture. Now he can do one of two things.

He can put you in a soft cast. Or he can put padding around the fractured metatarsal, and give you a Reese boot to immobilize the foot.

You'll be wearing one of these two devices—the cast or the boot—for a maximum of six weeks. That's how long it takes a stress fracture to heal.

A soft cast is made of gauze impregnated with zinc oxide paste. It never really gets hard, but it immobilizes the foot somewhat, and gives it some compression.

We don't like to immobilize the foot completely, because the muscle will start to atrophy. While you're wearing the cast, be sure you do some alternate exercise, like calisthenics that don't involve your foot, or weight lifting. A stationary bike or Nautilus machine is good. You don't want the rest of your body to suffer while your foot is healing.

The second method the doctor may use, instead of a cast, is to put padding under the adjacent metatarsals. For instance, if I believe that the second metatarsal is fractured, I pad the first and third metatarsal bones.

I take ⅛-inch thick felt padding and cut it about a ½-inch wide. I tape this along the two metatarsals next to the injured one. Now the injured metatarsal has a little groove to sit in. The pressure is taken off, and that gives you some relief.

Then I give the patient a Reese boot to wear.

About two weeks after your first visit, the doctor will probably have you come back for a second X ray. Now the stress fractures show up because they're starting to heal. And you know you've got four weeks to wait before you can get out of your cast or your boot and get back to running.

The medical world got a lot of experience with stress fractures during World War II. The army took civilians that had never done much physical exercise, put heavy packs on their backs and then had them march for miles.

Soon the rookies were complaining of foot pain. The doctors would take X rays and wouldn't see anything wrong with the bone. So of course, the GI's were accused of faking it. I think they called it goldbricking in those days. But the patient would keep complaining of severe pain, so two weeks later they'd take another X ray. And now they'd see some fuzziness along the periphery of the bone. Bone callus was forming; the healing process had started. That's how they knew it was a stress fracture. They called it March Fracture.

Today, runners get fractures of the metatarsal bone when they run long distances—like a marathon.

Ron Griswold is a tall, lean, hungry marathoner in great condition. He's a labor relations specialist who found that running is a great way to forget all the settlements and strikes and disputes and demands. Ron was about twenty-eight when he ran his first marathon—the 1976 New York City Marathon. He finished in an excellent time—three hours and forty-three minutes. He also finished with a metatarsal fracture. Ron was not my patient at that time.

I first saw him after the Yonkers Marathon in March 1977—with still another stress fracture. He told me that at the twenty mile mark, he felt severe pain over the instep. This time, he knew enough—and he hurt enough—not to finish the race.

Next day, he came limping into my waiting room, which was filled with all the other post-marathon casualties. Many runners seem to finish a marathon feeling sound and healthy.

It takes a day or two or three before they realize they've been injured.

And the opposite happens too. A runner will finish in great pain. But the podiatrists working at the end of the marathon advise him to use some first aid—like ice—and wait a few days. Very often the pain goes away as the body recovers from the stress of the long run.

Anyway, Ron was definitely injured, and he knew it. I felt his foot and found that the third metatarsal was extremely tender. Interestingly enough, it turned out to be the second metatarsal that was fractured.

I put Ron in a soft cast and Reese boot.

In about six weeks Ron started slowly running again. I made a mold of his foot and got him soft orthotics. He had been running in hard orthotics, and I felt he needed a softer surface to prevent further mayhem.

To no avail. Ron quickly built up his stamina, and ran another marathon in six months. You guessed it—he got another stress fracture, on the other foot—the left foot.

This time I put the metatarsal padding onto his orthotics and let him continue to run. Why? Because I couldn't stop him. Also, the pain wasn't as bad.

At this point I sent Ron for blood work-ups and a complete physical checkup—just on the chance there was something physically wrong with him. He checked out healthy as a horse.

So I realized that Ron must need extremely soft cushioning for races. I ordered a pair of what Dr. Schuster calls his pillows. They're made of a soft, cushiony material called Plastizote. It absorbs a tremendous amount of shock, and it feels like you're walking on marshmallows.

Of course, what you sacrifice is support. The pillows don't give as much support as regular orthotics.

At first Ron wore his regular orthotics for his day-in, day-out training. Then, for the hard stress of a race, he would run in his pillows.

Lately, he's given up the pillows and wears the orthotics

for both training and racing. Last time I heard from Ron he had moved to Washington, D.C. He's still running hard. And his metatarsals are holding up fine.

Pain between Ankle and Small Toe

(Cuboid pain)

This is the area of the cuboid bone, and pain here seems to be a symptom, not an injury in itself. We don't know the exact mechanics that cause this pain. But I do know that I always find it together with an arch that's collapsing. So if you have this pain, you should read the section on Weak Foot.

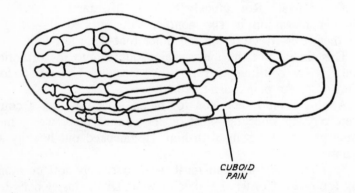

CUBOID
PAIN

You'll probably find that using a commercial arch support will help a lot. Many patients find the Arch-Supporting Strapping gives you a lot of relief. (Page 132.) Try these, and all the other techniques, exercises and running tips given for weak foot and you may be able to run comfortably.

If not, your podiatrist will have to look into what else is causing the pain.

Pain or Numbness from Instep to Toes

The subtitle to this "injury" should be "Tight Shoelaces" or "Tight Shoes." Because in most cases pain on top of the foot is caused by these two culprits.

Remember to buy running shoes in the afternoon, because your feet can swell a full size in the course of the day.

And be careful not to tie your shoelaces too tightly. This is easy to do, because your feet swell as you run—especially if you run long distances. You get interested in your speed and your mileage and very often you don't even feel the pain on top of the foot until you've stopped running.

This happened to Michael Douglas when he was in New York filming his movie, "Running." He was running a lot of miles and eventually developed neuralgia on the top of the foot. I gave him a doughnut pad to take the pressure off the painful area, and he bought looser shoes.

This may be the answer to your problem. Or you could try elasticized laces, which are sold in some orthopedic shoe stores. Or just take care to tie your laces a bit looser.

With some people, the problem is not just tight shoes. It's a bump on top of the foot—an enlarged bone, a bone spur. One of the small square bones in the middle of your foot has grown, probably because pressure was put on it.

All you do is take a foam rubber doughnut and place it over the bump before you put your sock on. Or some people like to glue the doughnut to the tongue of their running shoe, and that way they don't have to be bothered every time they put their shoes on.

If you've been putting pressure on that enlarged bone for a long time, nature may put a little padding around it—a pillow filled with liquid called a bursal sac. Pretty soon, with continued pressure, that sac will get irritated. Now you've got trouble.

Sometimes, your doctor will use injection therapy to bring the inflammation down.

The bone spur can be removed surgically, but to this day,

in twenty-seven years of practice, I've never had to remove a
bone spur surgically in that area. I'd rather find a way to
protect it from the shoe pressure.

Black Toenail

Runners are very prone to black toenail. It's caused by a
hemorrhage under the nail.

You can get this from wearing a short shoe. Or when you
run downhill, very often your shoe stops short and inertia
keeps your foot going forward inside the shoe. So you're
constantly jamming your nail against the end of the shoe.

You've got blocked-up blood under the nail. So you have
to let it out to relieve the pressure.

If the nail is black all the way to the end of the toe, take
a sharp razor blade and boil it fifteen minutes to sterilize it.
Now make a small cut in the skin directly under the toenail—
a slit maybe ⅛-inch long. It's absolutely painless because
that skin is blistered and blistered skin is separated from the
nerve endings. Don't do this if you're a diabetic or have cir-
culatory problems.

Let the blood out, soak the toe in nice hot soapy water, then
put a mild antiseptic on it. Betadine solution is probably the
best. Then cover it with gauze and tape the gauze down.

If the nail is black only at the base—not all the way to the
end of the toe, I'll tell you the method Bob Glover describes
in his book.

You take a paper clip and heat it up till it's almost red
hot and then touch the nail with the clip, being very careful
not to go too deeply. This melts the nail and lets the blood
out. Then you soak it in hot water.

I think Bob must have mellowed over the past few years,
because he says he'd never use the Burning Paper Clip
Method today. He'd go to a podiatrist.

So would I. I think it takes an awful lot of guts to put a
red hot paper clip to your nail. I don't know too many people

that have the guts to do it while they're sober.

What the podiatrist does is drill through the nail with a very fine dental type drill. It allows the blood to drain out, it's painless and it usually saves the nail.

You really have to take care of black toenail, because if you wait a week or two, the nail may start to crumble. If that happens, just leave it alone unless the nail is loose.

Loose portions of nail should be clipped away with a nail clipper. Then file them smooth so there are no sharp edges. Those edges can catch on your sock and you'll tear away the good nail.

Thick Toenail

(Onychogryphosis)

Nails can thicken to the point where they're ½-inch or ¾-inch thick. If a nail is that thick, the pressure of the shoe makes it very painful.

Thick nails are usually traumatic nails—nails that have been injured time and again. Either you've dropped things on your toe or you've been jamming your toes against the front of your shoe when you run.

There's nothing you can do about it except file the top of the nail or clip it from the top with a nail clipper to thin it down. Then smooth it out with an emery board.

Nobody said nails had to be filed and clipped only at the end. Just take an emery board and file it. Go back and forth carefully across the top until it's thin enough.

If you clip and/or file your thick nail, it has to be refiled periodically because it grows thick again.

A lot of podiatrists recommend removing the nail surgically so it never grows back. This eliminates a possible future problem. But it is painful and can keep you from running for from four-to-six weeks.

Once the skin has healed, it becomes thick and tough and

it looks fine. You can even paint the skin with nail polish.

But I prefer not to use surgery unless it's necessary and in this case it usually isn't. You can take care of your problem with just a few minutes filing when the toenail gets thick.

Thick, Discolored, Crumbled Nail

(Fungus nail)

This looks a lot like the thickened nail that the runner gets. But if your nail is also discolored—yellow or white discoloration, a mottled color—you've probably got a fungus nail.

Again, the nail can be removed surgically. Or the doctor might give you a drug to take orally. But, of course, any drug can have side effects.

The treatment I prefer is a combination of doctor's care and home care. First the doctor grinds away as much of the nail as possible. Then he gives you a prescription for either fungoid tincture or Onychophytex. Three times a week you buff the nail with an emery board to create a rough surface. Then you paint on the fungicide. Each week you remove the old fungicide with nail polish remover before putting on a new coat. This treatment takes nearly a year.

If your nail doesn't hurt, I like to try this conservative care. If that doesn't work, you can always remove the nail surgically. The nail doesn't grow back, but your skin toughens up and it looks okay when done surgically.

Ingrown Toenail

Most ingrown toenails are self-inflicted. You get one when a tight shoe presses on a nail that's been improperly cut or has a jagged edge.

How do people get jagged edges on their toenails? I say it's all the fault of television. Ninety percent of ingrown toenails wouldn't happen if it weren't for television.

People sit watching TV and unconsciously start picking at their toenails, sort of cleaning them. Not a very sexy sight, but what can you do? Some of the nicest people pick their toenails while watching TV.

In the process, they tear off a bit of the toenail and leave a jagged edge, like a hook. This hook is then pressed into the skin by a tight shoe, and the skin has a foreign body reaction. Your own nail becomes a foreign body to your skin.

Of course, this can also happen if you've cut your nails into V's or curves at the corners.

Once the nail is imbedded in your skin, you need professional help. Don't try to dig it out yourself. Let your podiatrist lift it up, cut it out and take care of the infection.

How to Cut Your Toenails

Cut your toenails straight across. Don't make V's in front of the nails, don't round the corners the way you do your fingernails.

How short should you cut them? Just cut them up to the end of the toe—where the toe begins.

If you keep your nails short and cut them straight across, you should have no trouble at all with ingrown toenails.

Blisters

The best treatment for blisters is to avoid them. Blisters are caused by something that's rubbing.

It could be a shoe that's too wide and moving from side to side. It could be a too-short or too-narrow shoe.

Abrasive socks can cause blisters. Nylon is often abrasive. I think you should wear only cotton or wool socks.

If you're running downhill, sometimes your shoe stops but

inertia keeps your foot moving. Then you get a blister on the tip of your toe.

You can get a blister on any prominence that sticks out and rubs against your shoe. For instance if you have a bunion, sometimes that rubs against a tight shoe and you get a blister. Or, the joints of your toes form "bumps." They can get blisters. People with hammer toes get blisters on the top of the toes and on the front end.

On the bottom of your foot, you sometimes get a blister along the arch, about a third of the way back, on the insole. This is because the first metatarsal is rolling in a bit and bearing too much pressure.

Bob Glover says rubbing Vaseline on your feet prevents blisters. Some people carry a tube of Vaseline with them on marathons to rub into their feet. That's fine, as long as you're not wearing soft orthotics. Vaseline soaks into the leather and separates the leather from the cork bottom. I think talcum powder is good. It reduces the friction and keeps your foot dry. Spenco insoles also reduce friction.

So your blister-prevention strategy has four steps: well-fitting shoes; nonabrasive socks; cushioning for any bumps on your feet; friction reducers like Vaseline, talcum powder or Spenco insoles.

If you get a blister anyway, leave it alone as long as it's small and painless. It's sterile as long as the skin isn't broken.

But if it's large and painful or it's interfering with your running, you can cut it open.

First sterilize a razor blade or nail clippers or scissors by boiling for fifteen minutes. Wash the blister with alcohol or Betadine or other antiseptic. Make a small slit in the blister and press the fluid out. This cut is painless, because blistered skin is not connected to the nerve endings.

Now clean the cut with antiseptic. Betadine solution is best. In my office, I also dry the area with 2 percent Gentian Violet, aqueous solution. The aqueous solution keeps it from burning. Your doctor can give you a prescription for this. Or you can buy 1 percent Gentian Violet without a prescription.

You want the blister to dry, so don't put ointment on it. Ointment doesn't allow for drainage; it dams up the wound. The skin can become macerated—wrinkled, white and soft.

Last, you cover the blister. I don't like Band-Aids because they're usually plastic and they don't allow air in. Use a square of gauze and put tape around the edges of the gauze.

At night take the bandage off and let the air at it.

The pain and throbbing will stop as soon as you let the fluid out. Don't peel the cap off the blister—it will flake off when it's ready.

Corns on Top and Sides of Toes

The only reason you'll ever get a corn on top of your toe is because the shoe is tight and it's rubbing. So get rid of the guilty shoe and take the pressure off the corn by using a little doughnut pad. If the shoe fits and the pressure's taken off long enough, the corn will disappear.

You can speed the process along by giving the corn a few strokes with an emery board two or three times a week. This reduces the size of the corn and therefore the pressure you get from the shoe. Also, it breaks the continuity of the hard skin and restores some flexibility to the skin.

I don't recommend cutting a corn with a razor blade. It's too easy to cut yourself. This is especially dangerous for people with poor circulation (that includes many diabetics) because the cut takes longer to heal and you're more prone to infection.

But if your circulation is good and you have nerves of steel and you're not afraid of the sight of your own blood, you can try cutting your corn. Be sure you boil the blade to sterilize it. And keep some antiseptic handy in case you cut yourself. Betadine is a good antiseptic.

One thing you should never do is use corn drops or pads impregnated with corn drops. Corn drops are basically salicylic acid, and they're a very insidious way to burn good tissue along with the corn tissue. Salicylic acid can burn the skin without your realizing it and even cause a hole, an ulcer on the foot.

If you happen to have bad circulation—which many diabetics have, as well as nondiabetics—salicylic acid can have serious consequences. If it burns or ulcerates the skin, your impaired circulation means slower healing and more chance of infection. New healing blood doesn't come in as quickly, and waste products aren't carried away as quickly. As a result, you have a good chance of infection and gangrene. You can even lose a limb.

You'll notice the bottle of corn drops and the package of corn pads impregnated with drops carry a warning for diabetics and other people with impaired circulation.

So I'd say, don't use them at all, even if you have good circulation. I'm not very happy with corn drops.

Corns between the Toes

(Soft corns)

These are called soft corns or heloma molle. They're no different from any other corn except that you sweat so much between the toes—runners especially. And the sweat softens the corns.

Very often they're misdiagnosed by patients and doctors and everybody else as athlete's foot because sometimes they happen way down in the web of the toes. The difference is, with athlete's foot you've got itching and scaling, while a corn is just a painful bump of tissue.

Sometimes a corn between the toes becomes infected by causing a foreign body reaction. It's a foreign body to your own skin. Or people scratch at a corn, and that can cause infection.

The only reason you'll ever get a soft corn is tight shoes,

narrow shoes. It's true, you are more likely to get any kind of corn if you have an enlarged bone—a bone spur—or an enlarged condyle on the bone. A condyle is a bump on the bone. It's a normal thing.

But that bone spur or condyle won't itself cause a corn unless your shoe is too tight.

So put your doughnut pad on the soft corn and don't wear any shoes that aren't wide and comfortable. If the corn is way down in the web of the toes, you can cut the doughnut pad in half and stick that on.

Don't use corn drops. And don't try to cut a corn between the toes with a razor blade.

If the corn's so painful you want to get it treated right away, let your doctor remove it.

Corns on Tip of Toes

Short shoes can cause corns on the tips of the toes. But basically they're the curse of people with hammer toes and people with the cavus type of foot.

The cavus foot has an extremely high arch and high instep and the toes are somewhat pulled back. The tendons on top of the toes are pulling the toes back. If you have this kind of foot, you get a lot of calluses on the ball of the foot. Very often you get corns on the tips of the toes and also on the tops of the toes.

Just use the doughnut pad and/or a metatarsal pad. And be sure your shoes are long enough. To relieve the callus on the ball of the foot, try a Scholl's Ball-O-Foot Cushion. Try it just as it comes. And also try cutting out a hole for the callus to go through.

Warts

A wart (or verucca) is another kind of lump on your foot.

Warts are caused by a virus, and they're contagious. You can spread them to yourself—so that one wart leads to more warts on your own body. And you can spread them to other people.

Warts grow in size. Sometimes they get so large and painful you can't walk on them.

Patients sometimes mistake warts for corns or calluses. But if you look closely, you can see that the center of the wart has little dark spots. These are small blood vessels and nerve endings. Corns have no blood vessels—they're just little lumps of dead skin. If you pinch a wart, you feel pain. Pressing on it is not so painful.

A wart bleeds freely. A corn doesn't bleed. Sometimes you cut a corn and it starts to bleed—but that's because you've cut the live skin underneath or around it.

Like corns, warts sometimes occur in spots where the shoe is causing too much pressure. They can also crop up in non-pressure areas. Warts on the bottom of the foot are known as plantar warts. Plantar refers to the bottom of the foot. Plantar warts are pushed deep inside the skin because of all the weight and pressure on them.

Warts are caused by a virus and they're contagious. I remember the time a group of my patients who were dancers in the New York City Ballet came back from a tour of the Southwest. About eighteen of them came into my office to be treated for plantar's warts. So it certainly seems that these dancers spread the virus to each other.

Yet I've never had warts, although I treat them and handle them all the time. So it must be that not everyone is susceptible to the virus.

Sometimes you get a whole cluster of tiny warts, and these are called mosaic warts. They form a mosaic pattern on the skin.

Some people try to cure warts by putting copper pennies on them, or using auto-suggestion or any number of folk remedies. Some of them work, sometimes. But if your wart isn't getting better, I think you should get to the doctor before you get more warts.

Don't try to remove a wart with drops. These drops are salicylic acid, and it's dangerous to use acid on your own skin. You often burn the good skin along with the wart.

The doctor may burn the wart off with chemicals or use electrocauterization or dry ice, or he can cut it out surgically. Some doctors inject vitamin A into the area. I don't know how successful this is.

There are a dozen different ways to treat warts, which means there's no good way. If there were a good way, everyone would use that and drop all the others.

No matter what method you use, there's a chance that the wart will recur.

When it comes to mosaic warts—small warts in clusters—the most successful treatment I've found is chemical treatment. Surgery doesn't seem to work because the warts keep recurring. I treat them in the office, and then give the patient some medication—possibly a drying agent—for home treatment. The patient comes back about once a month for a checkup and re-application of the chemical. This is a long process, and the patient has to cooperate fully and use the medication religiously.

Chemicals are the least painful method—especially when the removal is done slowly in many stages.

But the wart must be kept dry between treatments, and it's almost impossible for a runner to keep his feet dry.

What I prefer to do for runners is to inject Novocaine and remove the wart surgically. I tell the runner to come into the office after a big race—he needs a rest then anyway—and I remove the wart. You only have to keep it dry for about thirty-six hours. And in four or five days, your foot has healed and you're out running again.

Cracks between Toes

Cracking of the skin between the toes can be caused by athlete's foot, but not necessarily. With athlete's foot, you've also got itching and scaling.

Cracks can be caused simply by perspiration, and runners perspire tremendously. The moisture softens the skin and it cracks—especially during the winter months. Your feet are sweaty and suddenly they dry up in the cold and the skin cracks. It's very painful.

In the office I use 2 percent Gentian Violet on cracked skin, but you need a prescription for that. So what I recommend for home treatment is either 1 percent Gentian Violet or tincture of Benzoin compound. You can get these without a prescription. Dab the medication between your toes after you shower and powder your feet liberally after that. Also powder your feet before you go out running. The more you powder your feet, the more sweat will be absorbed and the less chance there is of cracking.

Cracks on Heels

Runners often get a lot of cracking around the periphery of the heels, especially in the winter when the skin is drier. But cracking rarely happens unless there's callus on the heel. So you may have to go to the doctor and have the callus removed. You can't really remove heavy callus with home treatment.

The doctor debrides the edges of the callus with a scalpel. Then he treats it with medication. He'll probably apply a bandage to keep the edges closed and promote more rapid healing. This treatment is painless and there's no bleeding.

If callus starts to form again after this treatment, you can use an emery board to remove some of the new callus. But don't overuse the emery board, or you'll rub your skin raw.

Stuff like Pretty Feet is nice, possibly for dry skin, but not for real callus. I don't think pumice stones do much either, except maybe exercise your arms. When a callus is really dry and hard, you'll take off a lot more with an emery board than you will with a pumice stone.

What I recommend, starting in the fall, is to rub a lot of

cream into your heels. There are a lot of good creams, and one hand cream is just as good as another. I tell all my patients to buy Spry or Crisco and rub that into the heels. It's cheaper than most creams and it works as well as anything I can think of.

Athlete's Foot

There are a few different kinds of athlete's foot. They're caused by different fungi, and they appear on different parts of the foot, and you need specific medications for each type of athlete's foot. A medication that works on the bottom of the foot may not work between the toes.

Usually you get athlete's foot between your toes—itching and scaling, sometimes even cracking between the toes.

This between-the-toes infection is usually a monillia type of infection. The powders don't do very much for it except to dry up the skin.

I would recommend you use liquids or creams. Some good products for the itching and fungus between the toes are Desenex Liquid, Lotramin and Enzactin Cream.

Athlete's foot can also show up on the bottom of the foot, again with itching and scaling and blisters. It rarely goes above the arch. A good preparation you can buy for this is Tinactin or NP27.

If the commercial preparations don't work, go to your GP, your podiatrist or your dermatologist and have him do a culture on it and find out what specific fungus is causing your problem and prescribe a medication for it.

All types of athlete's foot are contagious, and this means contagious to other parts of your own body—not only to other people. So be sure to dry your feet with paper towels, and throw the towels away, so you don't spread the infection.

Pain on Bottom of Foot, Arch and Heel

This pain could mean one or more of three injuries:
- plantar fasciitis
- heel spurs
- bursitis (inferior calcaneal bursitis)

They're all caused by the same actions on the bottom of your feet. To understand what's causing your pain, you have to know something about the materials that make up your foot.

When we started evolving our feet—transforming the ape's handlike foot into something we could stand and run on—nature looked around and came up with a variety of materials. She wanted to form a foot that would be rigid enough to stand on and flexible enough to bounce us along from one step to another.

So nature constructed the foot of hard things like bone and somewhat flexible things like tendons. And she used another interesting building material called fascia.

Fascia is used throughout the body to hold structures in place or as a separating material between muscle groups. Sometimes it's shaped into bands to connect one part to another—where you need a material that's firm but also flexible.

And that's what's needed in the arch of your foot. Fascia material is used here to make a somewhat flexible bridge from your heel bone to your toes. (Actually, to the heads of the metatarsal bones—the bones your toes are attached to.)

Okay, so this bridge—the arch of your foot—is made to flatten out a bit when weight moves across it. That's what happens when you run—the weight moves from the heel to the high curve of the arch and down to the ball of the foot. In a perfectly designed foot, the weight moves along a very specific path and the arch flattens a bit, then springs back up again as the weight moves off it.

But, if you have pain in the arch or the heel, it may be that your weight is taking the wrong lane across the bridge.

The bridge is stretched hard, and it hurts. It may even lose its flexibility, so it doesn't bounce back up again with each step. In this case we say your arch has "fallen."

Now three things can happen. Depending on just how your foot has responded, you've got one of three injuries.

First, you could have plantar fasciitis (pronounced fashee-itis.) This means the fascia has been pulled too hard, and it's inflamed. (The word plantar indicates the bottom of the foot.)

Second, you could have heel spurs. Some fascia fibers have pulled away from the heel bone, and droplets of blood were laid down. They eventually became calcified and formed an extra bit of bone, called a spur. You can see heel spurs on an X ray. They look like little points sticking out along the edge of the heel bone, where your arch starts.

Third, you could have bursitis. The heel has responded to the pressure by putting in cushioning right along the line where you've grown a heel spur. This liquid-filled cushion is called a bursal sac. If the pressure from the fascia continues, the sac itself becomes inflamed and sore, and you've got bursitis—inferior calcaneal bursitis. (The heel bone is the calcaneus.)

Very often, you've got all three injuries together. But we'll discuss them one by one.

Before we discuss each symptom, I want to give you some tips on all these bottom-of-foot problems. They're all aggravated by running on hard surfaces. By running on the balls of your feet, which you do during hill work or speed work. Or by excessive time spent running. No one can say what's excessive for you, but the foot damage is related to the amount of time you run.

Tight calf muscles and hamstring muscles make the strain on the arch even worse. Shoes that aren't flexible are another factor.

So look at your shoes. Be sure they're flexible at the ball of the foot. Then look at your way of running. Read chapter 2, "How to Run Right and Hurt Less."

And now let's look at your feet and see which injury you've got.

How to Tell Which Injury You've Got   Plantar fasciitis and heel spurs cause pain on the bottom of the heel. With both of them, you have pain after running, but not necessarily while you're running. (But some people with plantar fasciitis do have pain while running.)

With both these injuries, you have a lot of pain when you first get out of bed in the morning. Those first ten steps in the morning really hurt. I tell people with heel spurs not to try to stand the minute they get out of bed. The best way is to crawl to the bathroom and put your feet under hot water. Then you can walk.

Your feet may also hurt if you've been sitting a while and then stand up.

With plantar fasciitis, you can have pain all along the arch, or right at the front of the heel—where the heel meets the arch. Press anywhere along the arch, and it may hurt. You may feel a strain, a pull all along the arch. It may feel like the arch is tearing apart.

Here's how you tell the difference between plantar fasciitis and heel spurs.

With plantar fasciitis you feel pain when you press on the *middle* of the heel. Put your thumb there and press up—as if you could put your thumb through to the top of your foot.

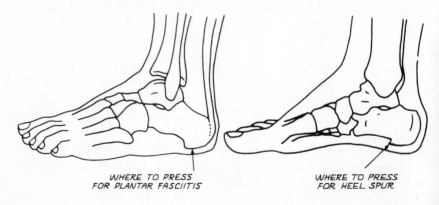

WHERE TO PRESS
FOR PLANTAR FASCIITIS

WHERE TO PRESS
FOR HEEL SPUR

With heel spurs, you feel pain when you press the *front* of the heel—where the heel meets the arch. Press backward, toward the back of the heel, and at the same time, press upward.

With bursitis, you also feel pain at the front of the heel. In fact, if you've got heel spurs, you probably have bursitis. It isn't the spur that hurts. That's bone, and bone doesn't hurt.

It's the inflamed bursa that's hurting. The treatment for these two problems is the same.

But first let's take the treatment of plantar fasciitis.

Plantar Fasciitis

This is an inflammation of the fascia—the tough, fibrous tissue that runs from the heel to the heads of the metatarsal bones.

Plantar fasciitis responds very well to home care. So try the various suggestions I'll give you here, and you can expect good results.

First step, as with any inflammation, is to ice the area. Put some ice cubes in a plastic bag and twist it closed. Then put the bag in a basin, and rest your feet on it. Ice your feet right after running—ten minutes on ice, ten minutes off, then repeat.

Also, you can take two buffered aspirins with each meal, if you're not allergic to aspirin, and don't have medical reasons to avoid it. Never take aspirin before running, because it masks pain—and pain is a symptom you should be aware of.

But to get at the cause of the injury, you'll have to change the weight distribution on your foot. As I explained earlier, when your weight moves across your arch, it's taking a wrong lane. And that misplaced weight is causing the irritation.

There are three things that can help a lot: an arch support; a heel pad to take some weight off the front of the heel; and strapping your foot to give support to the arch.

I suggest you try the Arch Supporting Strapping first. You need two materials: adhesive tape, 1½-inches wide. And Elastoplast, three inches wide. Elastoplast is like an Ace bandage with adhesive. A lot of drugstores carry it, or your druggist can order it for you.

The strapping is done in three steps. First step, encircle the outside of the foot with tape. Second step, apply tape from side to side, along the bottom of the foot. Third step, encircle the outside of the foot with tape one more time. This is to anchor the entire strapping down and keep the edges from raveling. (See illustrations for the first two steps.)

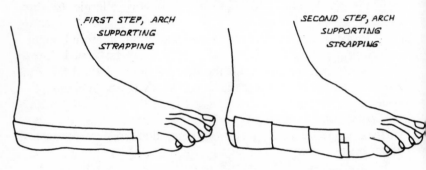

First step Attach the adhesive tape, starting right behind the bone attached to the little toe. Bring it around to the back of the heel. Lay it on gently, with no pressure.

As you make the turn around the heel, going toward the inside of the foot, give the tape a little tug so it's pulled tighter, from the heel to the inside of the foot. Anchor the tape at the ball of the foot just behind the big toe. Make the tape smooth—no wrinkles.

Second step Cut 3 pieces of Elastoplast, each about 4 inches long. Lay the first one along the sole of the foot, from just behind the little toe to just behind the big toe.

Overlap the second strip of Elastoplast, about ¾ of the way over the first. Then overlap the third strip. When you're putting tape across the bottom of the foot, hold the bottom of the foot to keep it smooth. The skin should not wrinkle.

Every wrinkle in the skin becomes a blister when you run.

Third step   Now take two strips of adhesive tape and tape down the edges, to anchor the entire taping down. Never wrap tape all the way around the top and bottom of your foot. This cuts off the circulation. When you run, the foot swells, and if you've cut off the circulation, the blood will be blocked in your toes, and you'll have Black Toe—not just Black Toenail. You can take a shower with this strapping—it will get wet and then dry off again. Change it after about three days. You'll only have to wear it about two weeks, and the pain should be gone by then. If the skin itches under the tape, remove the tape at once. You're probably allergic to the adhesive.

Along with the strapping, you can wear a store-bought arch support like Dr. Scholl's 610. This can be very helpful in raising the arch and taking a lot of weight off the heel. By raising the arch, you're shortening the distance between the origin and insertion of the plantar fascia, thereby taking some strain off it.

Remember, I told you there were three things that can help relieve your pain:
* strapping
* an arch support
* heel pads

You can wear the strapping alone, and see if that does it. Or you can wear the strapping and the arch support. Or you can add the heel pad and wear all three.

For a heel pad, use a piece of sponge rubber, ½-inch thick. Victex makeup sponges make good heel pads.

If you've tried all these and you're still in pain, throw away the heel pad and try a heel cup. This is a rubber or plastic cup you put in your shoe. When you wear it, your heel is falling into a trough, so again the weight is directed away from the arch. You can buy heel cups in a sporting goods store.

If you don't get relief from all these home treatments, see a podiatrist who treats athletes. He'll look at the entire weight-support system in your foot, and see how it has to be re-balanced. He'll probably design an orthotic insert for your shoe, and that will do the job.

Plantar fasciitis responds very well once your feet are given the right support. And it's worthwhile trying to do the job yourself. These home care treatments have a good chance of success, and you've saved yourself some money.

If you have plantar fasciitis, you can be one of many good runners who are having a fine time in spite of it.

One of these is Jane Killion, who was ranked eleventh in the world for women in the marathon event by *Track and Field News* in 1978. Jane was the third woman to finish the 1978 Boston Marathon. Her time was 2:47:22. She has also won three marathons, including the 1978 Finlandia.

Jane first came to see me after the Boston Marathon in 1977. She had started to feel pain during the marathon, but finished anyway. Jane had lots of problems, all arising from strain on the arch.

She had pain at the apex of the arch; a heel spur; and a plantar fascia problem which is fairly unusual. She had developed little nodules in the fascia that hurt when she stood or ran on them. They're very painful for a runner because they rub against the bottom of the shoe.

I made some orthotics for Jane to relieve the strain on the arch. And her orthotics have a trough gouged out for the nodules to sit in. If these nodules become troublesome again, we may have to remove them surgically. But so far, the orthotics have done the job fine, and Jane is moving right along as a world-class runner.

Heel Spurs and Bursitis

These two problems usually occur together, and the treatment for them is exactly the same.

First, let me give you the bad news: You probably can't cure your heel spur problem by yourself—but I will give you some home treatments to try. Maybe your case will respond to them.

Now the good news: Heel spurs can be treated very successfully by a podiatrist. It's one of the problems for which we can almost guarantee results.

All right, so you've read the beginning of this section. You know the symptoms and the test for heel spurs. And you've concluded that you've got them.

The first thing you should do is ice your heels after running. Put some ice cubes in a plastic bag and twist it closed. Put the bag in a basin and rest your feet on it. Leave your feet on the ice for ten minutes, then take them off for ten minutes. Then repeat.

Put heel pads in your shoes—pieces of sponge rubber, ¾-inch thick. If you can't find sponge rubber thick enough, use a couple of pieces. You can cut your own pads from a piece of sponge rubber or use Dr. Scholl's Heel Pads or Victex makeup sponges.

These heel pads will help absorb shock, and they'll help spread your weight over a greater area of the heel—so it's not all falling down toward the front where the heel spurs are.

You can try buying a running shoe with a thicker heel. Again, this gives you better shock absorption. And it puts the weight further forward on the foot; also relieves the tension on the plantar fascia.

Try Arch Supporting Strapping, or buy an arch support in the drugstore—Dr. Scholl's 610. Either of these techniques takes weight off your heel.

Now, after trying all these things, you'll probably get some relief. But in the long run, the problem will recur and become chronic, and you'll probably end up going to the podiatrist or orthopedist. I really don't think you can solve a heel spur problem yourself.

Your doctor will diagnose your problem as heel spur by pressing on the front of the heel, as I described. Then he'll probably X ray for confirmation of his diagnosis. Look again at the illustration showing you where to press for heel spur.

Notice the little point on the bone? That's how a heel spur looks on an X ray.

Some doctors may decide to use steroid injections in the heel or ultrasound. In my experience, these treatments can only give you relief for several weeks or a couple of months.

Ultimately, you're going to have to solve your weight-distribution problem, and that means an orthotic device made just for your foot and its own special problems. In our office, we make an orthotic that includes a cupped heel, a raised long arch and a redistribution of the weight so that the foot is completely balanced. The pressure is therefore taken off the spurs and shifted to other areas of the foot where it belongs.

Some doctors will do surgery and remove the spur. But I've never seen a heel spur that didn't respond to proper orthotic devices. Dr. Richard Schuster says that in his practice he has treated thousands of cases of heel spur and has never had to resort to heel spur surgery.

My experience is that after such an operation, you still have to wear an orthotic anyway. So save yourself an operation, just wear the device.

As I said earlier, heel spurs is one of the problems for which we can almost guarantee happy results—even though you may not believe it when you're hobbling along in pain.

John Pepowich was one of those unbelieving sufferers. He came to see me in January 1978, pretty well convinced that his running days were over.

John is about sixty-years old and he's secretary of the Masters Running Club. He came limping into my office and told me he had such pain in his arch and heel he could hardly walk in the morning. He virtually crawled out of bed.

X rays confirmed that he had heel spurs, and I fitted him for orthotics—doing my best to ignore the skepticism John was conveying in his eyes, his mannerisms and his voice.

The upshot of it is, I saw John crossing the finish line of a race not long ago. I assume he was wearing his orthotics. I know he was wearing a great big smile.

Weak Foot or Fallen Arches

*(Symptoms can be tired legs, pain in the arch, tiredness
in bottom of foot, low back pains)*

What used to be called flat feet is now called The Weak Foot
Syndrome or just weak foot. It can cause one or all of the
symptoms listed above.

The term "flat feet" is a little confusing because you can be
born with low arches or very high arches or "average" arches
and still develop the weak foot symptoms—because your arch
has been stretched so hard it's lost its flexibility. If you want
to understand how this happens, read the section just before
this one, "Pain on the Bottom of the Foot."

The simplest way to diagnose weak foot is simply to look
at your feet when you stand on them. With weak foot, your
weight falls in toward the inner side of your foot. Your arch
disappears to some extent. (In technical terms, the foot
pronates.)

Here's another way to tell. Stand up and put a pencil from
the first metatarsal head to the heel. If you have a normal
arch, the pencil runs straight between those two points. If you
have weak (pronated) foot, the pencil angles out from the
first metatarsal head.

Another test is to press on the arch—especially at the
highest point of the arch. That's very painful for people with
weak foot.

Another symptom of weak foot is not being able to walk
or run very far without getting sore, tired feet. Children with
weak foot tend to sit and watch, instead of running and playing. Johnny will act as second base instead of second base-
man because his feet are too tired.

Also, you can't stand very long without rolling your feet
toward the outside. I was discussing this problem with a new
patient, and she suddenly remembered seeing photographs of
herself as a child in which she was standing on the outer
edges of her feet. Her father used to tap her feet with a news-

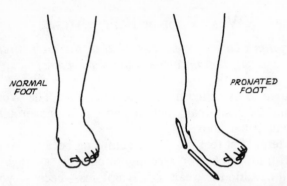

NORMAL
FOOT

PRONATED
FOOT

paper to remind her to get the weight back on the insides. But actually, she was making a right move, as children often do.

The inner side of the arch is weak, so people with this problem direct the weight toward the outside. This is a good exercise for you, by the way. And it's just what an arch support does—it tilts some of the weight toward the outside of the foot.

You can be born with high arches or low arches or "normal" arches and still develop weak foot symptoms. We've all got a pretty good shot at it.

Low arches are not an indication of problem feet. It's sort of a norn ᵃl "abnormality" and I wouldn't think of treating someone wiᴛh a low arch unless he were feeling weak foot symptoms. In fact, the low-arched foot may not show symptoms as readily as a foot with a very high arch.

Romance people—French, Italian, Spanish—tend to have high-arched feet, and these high arches can develop weak foot symptoms very readily because that high arch starts to strain under the stress of standing, walking and carrying weight.

Now you're running and maybe your arch has started to fall. But it might have fallen anyway if you're leading a normally active life.

Weak foot symptoms are helped by the Arch Supporting Strapping (page 132). Wear this strapping for a couple of weeks, until the pain is gone. At the same time, try Dr. Scholl's 610 Arch Supports. You should continue to wear these, even after the pain is gone. You can wear them while running too. This home treatment can very often solve your problem. If it doesn't, your podiatrist will have to analyze your whole weight-distribution problem, and probably design a custom-made orthotic for you.

And I want you to know that a lot of very strong runners have weak feet. Fritz Mueller is one of them. Fritz started running just a few years ago and he quickly became one of the world's best runners in the Master's class. (He's 43 years old.) He completed the 1978 Boston Marathon in 2:20:47.

Besides being a runner, Fritz is a chemist by profession and a bird watcher by avocation.

Fritz first came to me in 1977. His chief complaint was pain on the inner side of the ankle. I examined him and found another painful area at the highest point of the arch. Fritz felt pain while running and even when just standing on his feet.

He was wearing orthotics already, but at this point he needed more arch support. I sent his orthotics out to the lab for rebalancing, and meanwhile I gave him the Arch Supporting Strapping I just mentioned.

Fritz feels it was the strapping that solved his immediate problem, not the orthotics. He wore the orthotics only for training; for races, he ran without them. And he ran so successfully that he finished the 1977 New York City Marathon in a time of 2:27:25, setting a U.S. record for his class.

At the finish line he gave me one of the biggest thrills of my life by offering me his medal. I may not be much of a runner, but I sure love getting those medals!

Bump on Back of Heel

(Pump bump)

That bump on the back of your heel is probably something you were born with. Or maybe it developed under pressure or friction. It's called a pump bump or Haglund's deformity. It doesn't bother you unless your shoe keeps rubbing against it. Too much friction from the shoe can cause an irritation. The bump may even develop a bursal sac—a cushion filled with liquid. And then the bursal sac can get inflamed.

One reason why your shoe may be rubbing against the bump is that your arches are not solid when you walk and run. You may have the condition called weak foot—and you can read all about it in the preceding section.

If you do have weak foot, your foot may be giving a little twist every time you take a step. That's what's making the pump bump rub against your shoe.

Get some commercial arch supports, like Dr. Scholl's 610's, and that may solve your problem.

Another solution is to buy heel cups—cups made of rubber or plastic. You slip them inside your shoe. Next, put some cushioning inside the heel cup. To make the cushioning, get some foam rubber or felt padding and cut a U in it, so the bump sticks through the U. Put this padding inside the heel cup.

For my patients with pump bump, I make orthotics with a high padded back—it's built-up around the heel—and there's a U cut in it, so there's padding all around the bump.

Women can wear strap shoes or mules so the shoe won't press on the bump.

If it becomes very irritated, the bump can be removed surgically and this operation handles the problem very well.

Heel Bruise

Early in your running career you may get heel pains caused by inflammation of the coating on the bottom of the heel bone. Just ice your heels when you finish running. Put a plastic bag filled with ice cubes in a basin, and rest your heels on it for ten minutes. Then take them out for ten minutes. Do this two or three times.

Heel bruise seems to happen most often to new runners. The heel bone probably gets thicker and tougher as you run, and the pain gradually goes away.

Impact Shock

(New Runner's Injury)

Since long distance running has become so popular, doctors are seeing a new phenomenon called impact shock.

This problem happens most often to new runners or to experienced runners who've suddenly upped their mileage. If you're a new runner with impact shock, there are things you can do to decrease the pain. And you can also expect that it will take care of itself, as your body gets in condition.

Let's figure out just how much impact your body is absorbing.

Say you weigh 150 pounds and you run for just one mile. When you run, your heel hits the ground with three times your body weight. If you weigh 150 pounds, that's 450 pounds of impact, with each running step. And each foot takes from 800 to 1000 steps per mile. Four hundred fifty times 800 is 360,000 pounds you're socking into each heel in just one mile. And your heel is an area measuring about 1¼-inches in diameter. It's a wonder more people don't get impact shock.

The treatment for impact shock is to lessen the impact by cushioning the heel. Use sponge rubber heel pads. Victex makeup sponges are one good kind.

Try a different kind of shoe with an impact shock absorber. This is a shoe with a good deep heel. In between the outer sole and the inner sole there's a material that absorbs impact.

Shoes are very important in treating and preventing impact shock. Many runners wear heavier, better-cushioned shoes while they're training and then switch to lighter shoes for racing. These are called racing flats. They have less heel cushioning, less sole and more flexibility. Of course, for the long miles of daily training, they don't give enough cushioning.

Naturally, the overweight person is delivering more shock to his body than the lightweight runner. Dr. Schuster sometimes recommends that the overweight runner wear work shoes or combat boots to give better support and diminish the shock. Of course, you can't run a marathon in combat boots, but by the time you're ready to run 26.2 miles, you'll probably be a lot slimmer.

If heel cushioning and better shoes don't solve your problem, Dr. Schuster makes a kind of orthotic he calls his pillow. It's made of Plastizote, a very soft cushy material. Of course, inserts made of Plastizote do not give as good support as regular orthotics do. But if your main problem is impact shock, these pillows help a lot. A sports-oriented podiatrist can design one of these for your foot.

Impact shock can be very uncomfortable when you've got it, but as you adjust your shoes and your weight and your whole body, you'll find the impact pains will gradually go away.

Bob Anastasio is a 26-year-old runner who came to me with pains in front of the knees—one of the signs of impact shock. He certainly wasn't a beginner—Bob has run a number of four-minute miles—but he had been increasing his distance quite a bit.

Bob is basically a middle distance runner, and I think he was using long distances just to build up his stamina. But he was still wearing the light racing shoes he used for shorter distances, and they just weren't giving him enough cushioning.

I made Bob orthotics to correct some imbalances; and also added Plastizote to the heel, for extra cushioning. That was back in April 1977, and Bob hasn't had any impact shock problems since then—even though he runs about 75 miles per week.

Two months after he got the orthotics, Bob was the ninth American to finish the AAU 1500-meter championship in Los Angeles. His time was 3:43:07—roughly equivalent to a 4:01 mile. I didn't see that race—but I did see him finish a 1.7 mile race here in New York, right around that time. Bob ran with no pain, and finished in 7 minutes, 51 seconds. He walked away with the first-prize trophy—which he gave to me. You can bet it has a place of honor in my waiting room.

Pain on Bottom and Back of Heel, Young Person's Injury

(Apophycitis of the heel)

This injury can happen to children, up to age nineteen. Eleven-years old is the prime time.

The pain radiates up the back of the heel. If you clasp your hands around the heel and squeeze, there's extreme pain.

The heel bone, like many other bones, is still in two pieces before the age of nineteen. If the child has been jumping and landing flat on his heels, or running very long distances, the trauma can temporarily interrupt the closure line where the heel is supposed to fuse.

In Iron Curtain countries, where they've been a lot more scientific about studying and training their athletes, young teenagers are not allowed to run long distances.

If your child has this injury, tape his heel snugly. I'll tell you how to do the Heel Supporting Strapping I use. What you do is put one piece of tape around the back of the heel and one around the bottom of the heel—alternating tapes until you've formed a firm, supportive cup. Use 1½-inch wide adhesive tape.

1. Wrap the first piece around the back of the heel, from the inner ankle bone to the outer ankle bone.
2. Wrap the next tape around the bottom of the heel, from

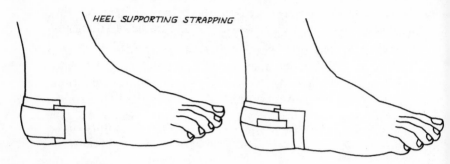

HEEL SUPPORTING STRAPPING

one ankle bone to the other. Wrap the tape snugly, as if it were helping to hold the heel bone on.

3. Put another tape around the back of the heel. Place it a bit lower than the first.

4. Put another tape around the bottom of the heel. Place it a bit more toward the back of the foot.

Use five or six pieces of tape, total. The last tape around the back of the heel should be down close to the sole.

At the same time, put sponge rubber padding in the heel of his shoes. He should wear this in all his shoes, and when you buy new shoes or sneakers, get them with well-cushioned heels. He should wear heel padding until he's nineteen.

Of course anyone who wears a heel lift in all his shoes may be shortening his Achilles tendon, and that can lead to other problems. But in this case, you have to take care of the main complaint, the heel injury. The child should do calf-stretching exercises to keep his Achilles tendons stretched out.

Another thing that can help is plastic heel cups, which you put in the shoes. You can buy these in sporting goods stores. He should wear the heel cups until he's pain free.

The separation will mend in six months, but the child should do no running or jumping during this period. This may sound impossible, but it's necessary, if the separation is ever going to heal. Swimming and bike riding are good alternate exercises during this period.

This same kind of fusion-line injury can happen in the metatarsals and shins. So I certainly would not let a youngster run long distances—no more than five miles a day.

Sprained Ankles and Broken Ankles

A sprained or broken ankle is not the sort of injury that sneaks up on you. If you've done it, you know it—because it happens suddenly.

The only question is—is it a sprain or a break?

You get one of these ankle injuries when you're running along a city street with potholes or a country road with holes and rocks and your ankle suddenly turns. The big toe and the heel turn in toward the center of the body. That's what causes an inversion sprain.

The pain radiates through the ankle joint, the foot and up the leg. There's going to be swelling, and the ankle might even be black and blue.

If you're like a lot of runners, you probably shake it off and keep on running—especially if you're in the middle of a race. You limp a little. Then when you get home, you do nothing and the ankle swells tremendously.

That's a serious mistake. The first twenty-four hours is the crucial time in caring for a sprained or broken ankle. Here's what you should do.

As soon as you feel your ankle twist and feel pain, stop running. Go right home.

Start your treatment as soon as you get home and continue it for the first twenty-four hours—or until you see a doctor. The first twenty-four hours is the crucial time for taking care of a sprained ankle.

Your treatment consists of ice and elevation. Put ice in a plastic bag and twist it closed. Put the bag on a chair and rest your ankle on it. Or put the bag on top of your ankle.

Keep your foot elevated as much as possible. In bed, put a couple of pillows under it. And keep using the ice—ten minutes on, ten minutes off—until bedtime.

In the morning, if your ankle is still swollen and painful, it's incumbent on you to go to the doctor. The chances are the doctor will x-ray, even though you don't think it's broken and he doesn't think it's broken. An X ray is a very important part of treating an ankle problem because very often there's a fracture at the base of the fifth metatarsal (the bone connected to your smallest toe) or a slight fracture of the fibula.

If you have a sprain, this means you've torn some ligaments —the nonelastic tissue that connects bone to bone. A fracture means you've broken one of the ankle bones.

In either case there may be internal bleeding. Your ankle may turn black and blue. The toes and the inner side of the ankle may even be black and blue because the blood sometimes seeps through the joint, so both sides of the ankle look bruised.

Whether you've got a sprain or a break, the motion of the ankle will have to be restricted. In fact, that's why your ankle swells. Swelling is your body's way of restricting motion.

If there's a break, your doctor will put the ankle in a cast. If you have a fracture of the base of the fifth metatarsal— which is a common fracture site when the ankle is twisted severely—the foot will either be put into a soft cast and a walking boot or in a hard cast. Your doctor will decide which method will work best for you.

If you have a mild sprain, the doctor may just put on an adhesive strapping or an Elastoplast strapping—depending on how much he feels the movement of the ankle should be restricted. Soft casts work well too.

But don't neglect an ankle sprain. It's one of the more neglected injuries. A lot of people just suffer through it and then the ligaments become stretched or completely torn, and you've got a chronic ankle sprain. This can mean you've got a mild degree of pain for a long time. Or it can mean you keep spraining your ankle again and again.

If I have a patient who keeps spraining his ankle, I give the ankle more support—limit its movement, really—by making an orthotic with a higher border on the outside of the foot, around the heel.

For someone who continually twists his ankle, Dr. Schuster worked out a great technique. You can get your shoemaker to do this for you. He takes a piece of Neoprene, ¼-inch thick, and glues it to the outer side of your running shoe, from the heel to behind the base of the fifth metatarsal. The Neoprene goes all the way from the upper edge of the shoe, down to the ground. Your shoemaker should taper the Neoprene so it's not so thick at the upper edge of the shoe.

Now the whole outer side of your running shoe is more solid so you can't twist in that direction. And the sole is a ¼-inch wider in that area. With this reinforcement on your running shoes, it's almost impossible for you to twist your ankle.

NEOPRENE WRAP
APPLIED TO SHOE

While we're talking about sprained ankles, I want to introduce you to one of my patients who is a typical sprained-ankle victim—she felt the pain but kept on running. Rosalie Prinzivalli is a 36-year-old runner who's been running about 3½ years and averages about 40 miles a week.

I'll let Rosalie tell her own story. This is taken from a tape of runners talking about their injuries—something runners dearly love to do.

ROSALIE: "Well, I had just recovered from my runner's knee injury and had that all solved. Then I started building up again, training for the New York City Marathon in 1978. It was my first long race in a while, so I was really looking forward to it.

My friend and I had barely started the Marathon—we were halfway across the Verrazano Bridge—when I stepped on a roll of candy and twisted my ankle.

I knew I couldn't finish the Marathon, but I didn't know where to go. If I turned around and went back to Staten Island, I thought there'd be no way to get home. (Runners always have some logical reason why they have to keep running on an injury.)

So I kept running forward, toward Brooklyn. My ankle didn't even hurt, as long as I didn't make any turns. I told my friend that when he stopped to put Vaseline on his feet, I'd ice down my ankle. They had ice at all the water stations.

So we got to Bedford-Stuyvesant, in Brooklyn, and I got some ice. When I looked at my ankle, wow, it was a mess. And once I stopped I couldn't start running again. But I'd already gone nine miles on a bad ankle. So I hitched a ride to the finish line and Murray was there working on everyone's feet. He taped my ankle and he didn't say much, but Shirley told me later (Shirley is Mrs. Weisenfeld) that he was very VERY upset that I'd run nine miles on a sprained ankle. He told me to ice it for ten minutes on, ten minutes off, for the next twenty-four hours, and I went to see him next day in the office."

That's Rosalie's story. Next day, the X ray showed that there were no broken bones. But she had torn a good many of the lateral ligaments. I put her in a soft cast for three weeks and kept her bandaged up for another two weeks. Her recovery is complete, but it kept her out of running for almost three months.

Isn't it miraculous that Rosalie was able to hitch a ride in Bedford-Stuyvesant, after she'd run nine miles—while it was absolutely impossible to find transportation back in Staten Island—a half mile away from her accident? Runners always have these very sound reasons why they have to keep running to the bitter end.

Lower Leg Pains

- Pain in Front of Leg: Anterior Shin Splints and Stress Fractures

- Pain on Inner Side of Leg: Posterior Tibial Shin Splints; Posterior Tibial Tendonitis; Stress Fractures
- Pain in Back of Leg, Just above Heel: Achilles Tendonitis
- Pain Midway Down the Calf: Soleus Muscle pain
- Sudden Pain in Back of Leg: Rupture of plantaris muscle

I can—and I will—give you a lot of bio-mechanical reasons why you're getting these various pains in the lower leg. But, for almost all these pains, there's one remedy: exercise to *stretch* the calf muscles and *strengthen* the front leg muscles. Most lower leg pains can be helped this way.

Also, you should check your running habits to see if they're contributing to your leg pains. Read the chapter "How to Run Right and Hurt Less."

First, here's a quick summary of the lower-leg pains listed above.

- Anterior shin splints are pain in front of the leg caused by inflammation of the sheath covering the bone, or by inflammation of the front-leg muscles (anterior muscles).
- Posterior tibial shin splints are felt on the inner side of the leg, between the calf muscle and the big shin bone. These shin splints are often related to fallen arches or weak foot.
- Shin fractures: Stress fractures of the shin are multiple micro-fractures of the tibial bone.
- Achilles tendonitis is a pain in the back of the leg, between the large calf muscle and the ankle bone. It's an inflammation of the tendon connecting the calf muscle and the heel bone.
- Soleus pain is a pain midway down the calf—higher up than Achilles pain. It means the soleus muscle needs some stretching.
- Rupture of the plantaris muscle is felt as a sudden sharp pain in back of the leg.

All right, now let's discuss.

What happens to your lower leg when you run? I've told you that most lower-leg pains come from a lack of stretching and strengthening—like it's all your fault. But to be fair, nature gave some people a head start toward lower-leg pains —because of the way she designed their feet and legs.

Maybe you have feet that don't stay steady when you run —they turn in or out, trying to find a balance. Since your feet are not stable, your legs have to work harder to add some stability.

Or, maybe you were born with short, bunchy muscles that are tight to start with—instead of long slender muscles.

I think the exercises you do as a child have something to do with the way your muscles develop.

And the environment you give your feet makes a difference. If you're a man who wears high-heeled boots, or a woman who wears high-heeled shoes most of the time, your calf muscles shorten.

There are many ways your environment can affect your leg muscles. For instance, if you have to be in bed for a week, be sure the blankets are lifted up off your toes. In the old days, the blankets were allowed to weigh on the patient's toes. The toes were pulled forward so the front leg muscles were stretched and the calf muscles became relatively shorter.

When the person got out of bed and stood up after a week, he'd say, "Wow, I'm really weak—I'm falling over backward." He wasn't weak, his calf muscles were shortened, and they were pulling him backward.

That's what's happening if you have lower-leg pains—your tight calf muscles are pulling on the weaker muscles in front of the leg. Actually every time you take a step, your calf muscle is pulling your heel up and pulling the front of the foot down. And that constant pulling can cause pain.

Running can give you pain on three different aspects of your lower leg—the front, the inner side or the back. Since these pains come from the same cause (tight calf muscles and weak anterior muscles), you may have more than one of these injuries at the same time. For instance, you'll very often have both Achilles tendonitis and shin splints.

Let's discuss the front of the leg first.

Pain in Front of Leg

(Anterior shin splints/stress fractures)

Okay, we said that pain in front of the lower leg can come from overworked anterior muscles and/or because the calf muscles are shortening and pulling the front leg muscles.

Why are those front muscles getting "overwork" pains, when the back muscles may not be? Usually it's because the front muscles are weaker than the posteriors. Running doesn't exercise them as much, so you need extra exercises. Do Foot Presses and Furniture Lifts to strengthen the anterior leg muscles. Do Wall Pushups to stretch the calf muscles. They're all described in Chapter 4.

Sometimes it's because you're forcing your front leg muscles to do a lot of other jobs besides running.

For instance, you may be running on a hard concrete road, and the padding in your shoes just isn't enough to cushion the shock. So your anterior leg muscles tighten up with every step, bracing themselves against that jolt. They're keeping the shock from spreading throughout the leg, hip and spine, but they're overworking with every step.

Incidentally, this may be the origin of the term "shin splint." Generally, to splint means to put a piece of rigid material near a hurt area and wrap some bandage around it. This restricts motion. So your anterior leg muscles are doing the same thing—they're acting as a splint and restricting motion from the foot.

What else could cause your front calf muscles to overwork? It could be that nature didn't issue you The Perfectly Designed Foot. Not too many people got that number. So your foot wobbles around a little, and the anterior leg muscles again do their tightening-up movement to add some strength and stability.

Some feet, in order to add stability, clutch with the toes. But of course they're clutching empty air, and that's tiring. Again, it's the front leg muscles that do the work because they control the toes. Some people are just wearing shoes that are too wide or too long, and that's why their toes are grasping and clutching. That one's easy to fix—just get smaller shoes.

Now you know what's causing the pain. What do you do about it?

If the pain is very bad, you should see your doctor right away to be sure you haven't got a stress fracture. A stress fracture isn't a sharp break, and you don't feel a sudden pain. It's many micro-fractures caused by continual strain, and the pain and fracturing build up gradually.

The only way to know you've got a stress fracture is to x-ray the area. Your doctor may take an X ray the first week you feel the pain and not see any sign of a fracture. Sometimes, his clinical intuition will tell him there's a fracture there anyway. So he'll have you stop running—just to be on the safe side—and ask to see you back in a week or two.

If I suspect a stress fracture of the tibia, I'll put the patient on crutches and send him to an orthopedist or an osteopath.

In about two weeks, some scar tissue starts to form along the lines of the fracture. That scar tissue does show up on a second X ray. Now the doctor knows for sure you've had a stress fracture. That means you can't run for another four weeks. If the fracture is bad enough, your doctor may decide to put you in a cast for a few weeks.

If your shin pain is moderate, you can try treating it yourself for a few days. It may simply be shin splints. But if you've stopped running, and followed all the suggestions I'll give you here for shin splints and the pain still hasn't decreased in a few days, you'd better see a doctor. Even a moderate degree of pain can mean a stress fracture, and your leg has to be put in a cast.

Now, here's the treatment for anterior shin splints.

1. First step is, bring down the pain and inflammation with an ice wrap. Before you go out to run, put a wet towel in the freezer. When you finish running, wrap the icy towel around your lower legs. Keep it there for 15 minutes. Put your feet

up on a chair while you're doing this. Or, use one of the commercial ice bags sold in running stores. They wrap around your leg and they're neater than a wet towel.

2. At bedtime, or any time during the evening, use a heating pad around the leg. Set it on low, never on high.

3. Take a couple of buffered aspirin at mealtimes and bedtime. Never before running.

4. Take a look at your feet, when you're standing on them. Are the arches flattening out? If you have painful arches, or any other symptom of weak foot, read that section and treat yourself for weak foot.

5. Cut down on your running. Cut it out for a while, if necessary. Don't try to run through the pain. You'll never get through it, you'll just make it worse.

6. Whenever you have to give up running for a while, the best exercise is swimming. And here's a good exercise while you're in the water—put an inner tube under your armpits to keep yourself afloat in a standing position. Now "run" in the water. You're using your running muscles, without putting any body weight on your legs.

7. I told you that your toes may be clutching, reaching for support, as if they were fingers. But they're clutching empty air, and that can cause strain on the anterior leg muscles. Okay, put something under the crest of the toes so they're not grabbing empty air. Get a crest pad in the drugstore. Put this padding under the three middle toes.

If you can't find crest pads, get some moleskin, about three inches wide. Roll it into a tube. Use enough moleskin to make a tube of ¼-inch diameter. Wrap this in gauze to hold it together.Now tuck it under the three middle toes and wrap tape around all three toes, including the padding.

Another good padding is the cotton sticks your dentist uses. See if he'll give you some of those.

8. Check your shoes. Sometimes a more solid shoe, with better cushioning and a better heel lift, can make all the difference.

One of my patients, Mitch Maslin, cured his shin splints by changing shoes.

Mitch is one of the "too much, too soon" school of runners who suffer all kinds of injuries because they can't resist the call of the road.

Mitch watched the New York City Marathon in 1976 and was filled with a flaming determination to be running it in 1977. In Mitch's own words: "In two months I ran myself into the ground."

So he went through many months of pains and treatments and sitting on the sideline while his various injuries healed and then going out running again. Finally, before the 1977 marathon, he was suffering with shin splints, but he insisted on running the marathon, against my advice and everyone else's advice. He finished the marathon with a stress fracture, which eventually healed.

Then, when he returned to running, Mitch discovered that just three short outings brought on a return of shin pains. He had shin splints. We tried all sorts of cures, like heel lifts and variations in the orthotics—with not much success. Finally one day Mitch decided to buy some new shoes and almost overnight the shin splints disappeared.

In comparing his shoes (like a lot of runners, Mitch has about eight pairs), he noticed that the new shoes were wider across the arch and ball of the foot. So he concluded that the greater stability is what he needed. I think the heel lift is what did it—that particular shoe, the Brooks Vantage, has a good high heel lift. Maybe it was a combination of a higher heel and a wider base.

So the right shoes are important. But another important moral I want you to learn from Mitch's story is how much of your pain can be self-inflicted. It can come from too much mileage—from not listening to your body when it first starts to hurt.

And it can come from improper running style. When you get back to running, be very aware of what could be causing your injury. Run on dirt instead of concrete. Avoid too much hill work and speed work, because they keep you running on the balls of the feet.

Check your running posture. Your weight should be directly over your hips. Don't lean forward. That's to avoid pulling too hard on the calf muscles. Read chapter 2, "How to Run Right and Hurt Less."

This is how you work with your body and give it the conditions it needs, the strength and flexibility it needs to keep your running a pleasure.

But suppose you've done all these good things—including wearing a commercial arch support, as recommended in the weak foot section—and you've still got pain in the shins and along the outer side of the leg?

You may have a foot imbalance problem that your commercial arch supports just weren't made to handle. Your foot is about as individual as your fingerprint. A mass-produced foot support may do the job for you. Or you may need a podiatrist to analyze just how your foot is made, and how it functions when you run.

A sports-oriented podiatrist can do this, and design a support that keeps your foot from turning in or keeps the arch from flattening or keeps your toes from clutching—or any combination like that.

Pain on Inner Side of Leg

(Posterior tibial shin splints or tendonitis; stress fracture)

You feel this pain deep inside the leg. Press the inner side of your leg—the line between the calf muscle and the big shin bone. If that's painful, you've put some strain on a muscle that runs from the shin bone around the ankle and attaches behind the ball of the foot. This muscle gives some support to the arch of the foot.

Most likely, your arches "fall" when you run. Read the section on weak foot, and follow those procedures—the arch supporting strapping, the commercial arch support and the heel pads.

You should also do stretching exercises to stretch the calf muscle. Wall Pushups is a good one. And your first aid is the same as for anterior shin splints. Wrap your leg in an icy towel after running. Take two aspirins with each meal. Don't try to run through pain. You've got to rest.

These procedures will relieve the pain of tendonitis or shin splints. They will not help a stress fracture. So, if you've strapped your foot and you've taken a few days rest from running and the pain is still not relieved very much, you have to assume you have a stress fracture. Another symptom of stress fracture is much more severe pain than you'd get with tendonitis or shin splints.

If you do suspect a stress fracture, go see an osteopath or an orthopedist and let him take care of it for you. He'll x-ray to confirm the diagnosis and probably put you in a cast and on crutches to immobilize the area.

Pain in Back of Leg above Heel

(Achilles tendonitis)

The Achilles tendon is a cord connecting the heel to the calf muscle. If you feel pain in that lower part of the calf—near where the cord is attached to the heel—you probably have Achilles tendonitis.

Here's the first thing I would do, if you came into my office. You can do it yourself, now. With your thumb and forefinger, pinch along the Achilles tendon. Start down close to the heel and continue pinching, working your way up to

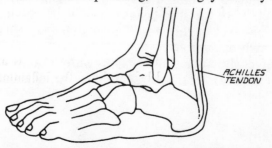

ACHILLES TENDON

where the tendon enters the calf muscle. If you feel a little swelling there, and a lot of pain, you've got Achilles tendonitis.

Here's what's happening inside your leg. The Achilles tendon is a cord connecting your calf muscle to your heel. Actually, it's a cord inside a tube. This cord and its tube (sheath) stretch a bit, but not much. So if anything pulls too much on either end of that tendon, you're going to start feeling a lot of pain.

What happens is the fluid between the tendon and its sheath expands, and there's less space for the tendon to move in. It all feels sore and swollen.

What's pulling on this tendon? There are two possibilities: a calf muscle that's too short (running shortens the calf muscle); and a heel that's too far away from the calf muscle.

What to do About It   When you realize this, you can see that the first solution is quick and easy: Put something under your heel to lift it up so it won't be pulling down so hard.

Just stick a piece of sponge rubber, about ¾-inch thick, in your shoes. Victex makeup sponges are good. The same stuff is sold under the name JogHeel. But it doesn't have to be any particular brand—just take a piece of sponge rubber and shove it under your heel—in your running shoes and your daytime shoes. This is going to help a lot right away.

Women can wear high-heeled shoes during the day, and that's a help. But once you've corrected the tendonitis, I don't recommend high heels—they keep your calf muscle short.

The next prescription may be a little tough to take, but you've got to do it. Stop running for a few days to a couple of weeks until the pain is a lot better. Later, do the Wall Pushups described in chapter 4. That's the most important part of your cure. But don't start these right away. Don't run, don't stretch for a while. Your tendon has been pulled too much already, and your muscle can go into spasm if you pull it any more.

A quick treatment you can start right away is an ice pack —it relieves the pain and brings down the inflammation. You can use the ice packs sold in running stores, they're probably the neatest. Or you can put a wet towel in the freezer for a half hour, and wrap that around your legs for fifteen minutes.

When you go back to running, ice the tendons after each run, but not until you've done your stretching exercises.

At other times of the day, I would put a heating pad on the area to improve circulation and bring some blood to the area. Do this while you're sitting around the house doing paperwork or watching TV. Also at bedtime. It will help get the swelling and inflammation down.

You can also take a couple of buffered aspirins to bring down the inflammation. I'd say two aspirins at each meal and two at bedtime. But don't take aspirin before running, because you deaden the pain—and that could be dangerous. Of course if you have ulcers or you're allergic to aspirin, don't take them.

Stretch Those Calves! Stretch Those Hams! Almost every famous athlete has had Achilles tendonitis at one time or another, because the more they work at their sport, the more they tighten and shorten the calf muscles and hamstrings.

The hamstrings are the muscles in the back of your thigh, between your knee and your butt.

You've got to stretch the calf and hamstring muscles. Wall Pushups will stretch the calf muscles. Knee Press and Foot on Table will stretch the hams. Squats will stretch the Achilles tendon. All these exercises are in chapter 4 and they're easy to learn. Do them before and after running. If you forget, your Achilles tendon will remind you.

Now check your shoes. If you've got Achilles problems, the two most important things to check in your running shoes are the heel lift and the flexibility at the ball of the foot. The heel should be ¾-inch thick. Read chapter 3 to evaluate your present shoes, and guide you when it's time to buy new ones.

What your foot's doing to your tendons. The structure of your feet may make you run in ways that put extra strain on the tendons. If the right shoes and plenty of stretching don't give you a complete cure, a sports-oriented podiatrist can tell you if your foot is contributing to the problem. Orthotics made to your foot's mold can correct any imbalances and ease the strain on the tendons.

And take a good look at your running style. So far, you've learned something very valuable: too much pull on the tendon while you're running is what's causing the pain. Where you run and how you run makes a big difference in the amount of pull on the Achilles. So read chapter 2, "How to Run Right and Hurt Less," to see how you can improve your style and your comfort.

If I had to pick one running habit that's most harmful to your Achilles tendons, I'd say it's running uphill. Cut out hill work until your problem clears up and your calf muscle is elongated.

Cutting the cord. A few very rare people will still be suffering, even if they've taken all the steps discussed above. You remember, a tendon is a cord inside a tube or sheath. Well, sometimes adhesions form, and the cord gets attached to the sheath. Then the cord can't move. These adhesions can be removed surgically to allow the tendon to glide normally.

Or sometimes a bone with a sharp bump may be sticking into the tendon. Surgery can take care of this too.

But surgery on the Achilles tendon still has a lot of unknown territory. Don't consider it unless you've really done your homework—stretching, shoe adjustment and adjustment of your running conditions.

Pain in Mid Calf

(Soleus muscle pain)

Soleus pain is a dull aching pain you feel midway down the calf, rather than down low near the heel. (Pain in the lower calf, near the heel, is Achilles tendonitis.)

The soleus muscle comes between the two heads of the big calf muscle. When you use your calf muscles, the soleus is the one that acts first. It moves maybe a thousandth of a second before the large calf muscle. So it does take a beating. It tightens up and gets sore, and there's a good exercise for it which you should add to your regular wall pushups. After your wall pushups, keep your feet flat on the floor. Now dip one knee a little, and you're stretching the soleus muscle. Hold for 5 seconds. Repeat with the other leg. This exercise is illustrated in chapter 4.

Ice your legs after running with a wet towel you've chilled in the freezer. Use a heating pad at night—on low, never on high. Elevate your heels with heel lifts inside your running shoes and your everyday shoes. Do a lot more stretching, but don't stretch while the pain is in the acute stage. No hill work or speed work until the pain is gone.

In fact, you've got soleus pain for the same reasons you would get Achilles tendonitis. So read the section on Achilles tendonitis and follow the same treatment.

Sudden Pain in Back of Leg
(Rupture of plantaris muscle)

I can tell when a patient has ruptured the plantaris muscle because he'll say, "I was running along, and I thought someone hit me with a rock." Golfers will say they thought they were hit with a golf ball, and a tennis player will think that her doubles partner hit her with a tennis racket.

You get a sudden, excruciating pain, and it's difficult to bear weight on the heel. You have to walk on the ball of the foot. You may get a black and blue mark running down the back of the leg from internal bleeding.

The plantaris muscle is a thin muscle, about as thick as a rubber band. It runs down the middle of the calf and attaches near the Achilles tendon.

This muscle doesn't seem to do very much so a rupture is nothing to worry about. Either the muscle repairs itself or you get along without it.

Just keep your leg comfortable for a couple of weeks. Use a heating pad in the evening to bring healing blood to the area. Women should wear high-heeled shoes to relieve the strain, and men can wear some of those fancy high-heeled boots that are popular now.

Or you can put padding under your heels, in your regular shoes. (Put the padding in both shoes, or you'll give yourself some of the problems that go with Short Leg Syndrome.) Use sponge rubber makeup sponges or heel pads that you can buy on the foot care rack. You can go to your podiatrist and he can strap your foot to keep it in an extended position. That gives relief.

But usually all you have to do is raise the heel and of course don't run until the pain is gone, which is about two weeks.

Knee Pains

The most common knee pain among runners—in fact, one of the most common runner's injuries—is runner's knee. The symptom is pain on either side of the knee.

A less common knee problem—but it does happen to athletes—is pain and swelling in the back of the knee, toward the inner side of the leg. This is a growth called Baker's cyst.

Let's take runner's knee first.

Pain on Either Side of Knee

(Runner's Knee)

I don't believe in predicting injuries for my patients, but if you're going to get any injury, runner's knee is a great possibility. This injury is very common with all kinds of "running" athletes—runners, tennis players, basketball players. One of the running magazines polled its readers and found that 23 percent of them had been put out of the running by knee problems.

Runner's knee can happen to beginning runners. But very often, the symptoms start when you reach thirty-eight or forty miles a week. One day, when you're three or four miles into your run, you feel pain either on the inner side or the outer side of your knee.

Maybe you stop running and rest for a couple of days. Next time you go out, you've only run a mile or two, and your knees start hurting again. And the pain has increased in intensity.

Some runners feel pain, not during the run, but later that day or next morning.

You may find that the pain is worse running downhill than it is when you run uphill. And it's worse when you walk down the stairs than it is walking up the stairs.

Or, after sitting a while in a movie or in a car, you find that your knee is stiff and painful when you walk on it again.

Take your own "running history" just as a podiatrist would do if you went to see him to see if you've been having symptoms like this. A good way to review your recent running is to talk it over with a friend. That often helps you remember the details.

One question you should ask yourself: Have you been running on a banked surface? If so, you're giving yourself one "short leg" and one "long leg." This often leads to runner's knee symptoms. In fact, you may really *have* one short leg— so compare your leg lengths, following the instructions on page 88.

Some more questions to ask yourself: Did you increase your mileage drastically just before you started feeling knee pains? Had you been doing a lot of hill work or speed work? All these questions will help you find the reasons for that knee pain.

After you've taken a good look at your running history, here's an examination you can do. I always use it when I suspect runner's knee. You'll need a friend to do my part in this examination.

Sit down in a chair and stretch one leg out straight, supporting your foot on another chair or low table. Your "podiatrist" now squeezes your leg just above the knee. At the same time, he uses his other hand to push on the kneecap. He pushes on the outside of the kneecap, pushing it toward the center. At the same time, the patient should tighten up his thigh muscle. If this test causes pain, you've got runner's knee.

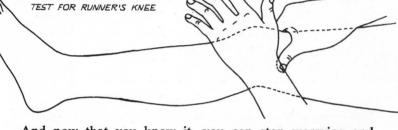

TEST FOR RUNNER'S KNEE

And now that you know it, you can stop worrying and start working—because runner's knee can be treated very successfully—and most of the treatment comes from you. Your own body causes the problem, and you've got to make the changes in your body that will cure it.

Not too many years ago, runner's knee was treated by surgery—taking out some of the rough, inflamed cushioning material around the knee (the cartilage), or by smoothing it down. This didn't work too well, since you need that cushioning when you run. So the pain would return soon after you resumed your sport.

But no sports-oriented podiatrist or orthopedist would think of surgery for runner's knee today. Because the simple and encouraging truth is, if your feet and thighs are doing their job right, you'll have no trouble at all with your knees.

We'll explain more about that later. But first let's give you some quick relief and reassurance.

First Aid   Ice the knee for fifteen minutes after running. Prepare your ice pack just before you go out to run by putting two wet towels in the freezer. After you run, wrap these towels around your knees for fifteen minutes. The pain is numbed, and the inflammation is decreased. One of my patients decided to be very efficient and leave the wet towels in the refrigerator (not the freezer), all day long so he could use them more frequently. This causes a very smelly refrigerator, so I don't advise it.

At bedtime, you can use heat on your knees for a half hour —a heating pad is fine, or warm wet towels. Wet heat and dry heat both work fine.

You can also take two aspirins with each meal and two at bedtime to decrease the inflammation. Please don't take aspirin before running because it can deaden the pain. And that's dangerous. I'd rather have you know what's hurting you and how much.

Long Range Cure   Okay, you've brought the pain down. Now let's get to the cause of your pain and get rid of it. I mentioned before that runner's knee comes from your feet and thighs. So you've got to do two things: Support your feet; strengthen your thighs.

Support your feet.   If you've got runner's knee, your foot is probably built in such a way that it makes a wrong movement every time it hits the ground. And it hits the ground very frequently when you run—with a lot of impact. Your foot may flatten out when you run—or turn out too much—or rock from side to side. This makes your shin bone move wrong and your knee move wrong. Those wrong moves are what's causing the pain.

Incidentally, you don't have to have "flat feet" or "fallen arches" to get this problem. When you run, you're asking your foot to do a highly complicated job. It has to take the impact of landing on the heel with three or four times the weight of your body. Then it must support you in a stable position for a fraction of a second. Then it must propel you off the ball of the foot with a bounce. With so many different demands put on it, there are lots of ways your foot's structure can fail.

So you've got to keep the foot from making these wrong moves. How? With a corrective foot support.

Try a commercially made foot support, which you can find in your drugstore. There are lots of good ones—Dr. Scholl's 610 is one. If this gives you some relief, you can be pretty sure your knee problem starts with your foot structure.

Here's another way to tell whether your knee pain is starting in the knee itself or in the foot: If the pain started almost as soon as you began running, it's probably a problem in the knee itself. If the pain started after you'd been running a while, it's probably caused by a foot imbalance.

Okay, so you've got your foot supports from the drugstore. And now you add the exercises I'll give you for strengthening your front thigh muscles. And that may be the end of your knee problem.

If not, you may need a better correction of your foot-balance problem, and you can get that with custom-made orthotics. A sports-oriented podiatrist can make a pair for you, from a mold of your foot.

Will the proper foot support cure your runner's knee? Absolutely not—not by itself.

Strengthen your thighs.   You've got to strengthen your thigh muscles so they can hold the kneecap in place—not let it twist to the side—when you're running. Turn to chapter 4, and learn the Quadriceps Exercises. We give four or five exercises, but pick two and do them conscientiously and that will do the job.

Runner's Knee—How Did It Happen to Me?   Nature gave the knee cap a very precise path to follow in life—a nice little

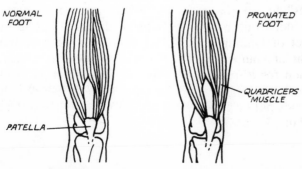

NORMAL FOOT

PRONATED FOOT

QUADRICEPS MUSCLE

PATELLA

groove in the thigh bone where it can move up and down smoothly and comfortably. You've got runner's knee because your kneecap moves out of its groove.

It twists and moves at an angle over the knob of the thigh bone. This twisting and bumping happens about 800 times in a mile of running. That hurts.

Soon the cushioning material (cartilage) around the kneecap gets worn and uneven. The medical name for runner's knee is chondromalacia of the patella (chondro—cartilage; malacia—softening; patella—kneecap).

And that wrong movement starts with your foot, as I explained earlier.

Now, how does the thigh contribute to your troubles? As you run, the four muscles in the front of the thigh (the quadriceps) should be supporting the kneecap so it rides up and down in its groove (not at an angle). But weak quadriceps allow the kneecap to pull and twist to the side, and irritate the cartilage.

How could I accuse a healthy, athletic person like you of having weak quadriceps?

I'll tell you. There must be a *balance* of strength among your thigh muscles, or the whole thing doesn't work right. If the muscles in the back of your thigh become a lot stronger than those in the front, you're in trouble. Those front muscles become the weak link. And this is just what you've done, with all that healthy running.

Running develops the back thigh muscles more than the front. So now you've got (relatively) weak quadriceps. And the more you run, the more you've got to strengthen the quadriceps.

Now Check Your Running Habits   Your running style is very much influenced by how your foot is built. That's natural. Maybe your foot structure is causing you to turn your toes outward too much, giving a twist to the shin bone. Try toeing in a little as you run—this can help relieve the pain. Your podiatrist can check your running style and point out any habits that are causing you pain.

Another thing is, where do you run?

If you're running on the side of the street—where it slopes—you're automatically giving yourself one leg that's shorter than the other. This "short" leg—the upper leg—is turning in and down (pronating) and is more likely to get runner's knee symptoms. So if you must run on a slope, be sure that your legs take turns being the "short" leg. Better yet, run on a flat surface.

Indoor tracks are the worst. On a short track, you may be circling thirty to forty times a mile, and you're constantly turning one foot down. Even if you alternate directions frequently, it's not the best place to run. I know it's hard to run outdoors in the middle of a Chicago snowstorm, but if you've got knee problems, an indoor track is not the place for you. Try it, and if your knee problem flares up, consider some other sport for the winter.

Some runners are getting interested in rope-jumping, but I don't recommend it. You're pounding down on the metatarsals, and causing a lot of trauma. And jumping on the balls of the feet can cause Achilles tendonitis or shin splints. If you really love rope-jumping, do it on a padded mat. That helps.

An aerobic sport I do recommend is indoor swimming. Try that until the weather or your knees clear up, whichever comes first.

There used to be a saying among athletes that knee problems were almost incurable. "You think you've got it licked, and it comes back next season!" Well, this may be true of some knee injuries. But runner's knee can definitely be licked, if you do your quadriceps exercises with massive determination.

Some of the most energetic runners I know are lazy about doing their quadriceps exercises.

On the other hand, some patients become fanatic about doing their exercises. One of my runner's knee patients is Dr. Enrique Loutsch, a psychoanalyst who started running because he felt it would help him give up cigars.

The first few days he would run just a few yards on the beach and then he'd feel his heart pounding and he thought he was about to die. But day by day his heart started pounding easier, the urge for cigars went away, he was happy as a clam—and his knees started killing him.

Enrique is like a lot of runners—I think many of them are males—who have a great belief in will power. He felt pain in his knees, so what should he do? Run through it! Use will power! He kept running and walking up and down flights of stairs.

The pain got worse and he couldn't sleep and his knees hurt even when he was sitting down. So he rested a few days and then went out to the country and ran a mile—up and down hills. The worst thing he could have done. He was heartbroken because he believed in the great myth of Incurable Knee Injuries, and he thought he would have to give up running.

Finally a friend persuaded him to come see me, and he came—early in 1978—with great skepticism. Enrique has weak foot, and he had been wearing arch supports for years —but they didn't happen to do the job for running. I prescribed some orthotics for him and told him to write himself a prescription for Butazolodine and taught him the quadriceps exercises.

He went home full of pain and skepticism. But then the idea of curing his pain through exercise seemed to appeal to his will power. He became a quadriceps-exercise fanatic and today he's in heavy training for this year's marathon.

Pain and Swelling behind the Knee

(Baker's Cyst)

This is an athlete's injury. Runners and tennis players get it. You feel pain at the junction where the upper leg meets the lower leg in back. It's fairly painful when you're running.

Reach back and feel it, and you can feel a lump, like a little ball of gelatin.

This is a non-malignant growth, and it's not something you can treat yourself. Go to an orthopedic surgeon, and have him take care of it for you.

Pain in Upper Inner Thigh Muscle

(Groin pull)

You get this pain from tensing up the inner thigh muscle (the adductor muscle). The adductor muscle is involved with turning the toe in, which is something you normally do when you run. Stretch your leg out and put your hand on the inner thigh muscle. Now turn your toe in. You can feel the movement in the adductor muscle. When you overwork that muscle, it can become tense and painful.

If you've been running on slippery streets—after the snow or rain or on wet leaves—you may feel pain on the inner thighs. You've been tensing up, trying to keep your balance. A friend of mine got groin pull in the right leg after spending a Sunday playing soccer with his son. He kept turning his toe in and tensing up the inner thigh muscle every time he kicked the ball.

Some people tense up this muscle because their feet are not balanced properly. If there's not enough lateral movement of the heel and ankle, the adductor muscle tightens up to help balance the body. The answer to this problem is to help the ankles and heels turn out. We do this by putting a wedge under the inner side of the heel. With this artificial eversion, the heels turns out the way it's supposed to, and there's no special strain on the thigh muscles.

If you have a groin pull, the shoes you wear can make a difference. Don't wear shoes with a very flared heel. That's a heel that's a lot wider at the bottom. The wide base may restrain the lateral movement of the heel and ankle.

Before I tell you how to treat groin pull, I want to mention another type of pain in the groin area that women sometimes get. I see about four cases of this a year. The pain starts high up on the inner thigh, so the patient thinks it's groin pull. But then, after a few days, the pain appears right under the groin—in the bottom of the pelvic bone. In this case, you may have an ischeal fracture (the ischeum is part of the pelvis), and you should see an orthopedist and have an X ray to check on it.

Now let's discuss the treatment of groin pull. If you're in pain now, cut down on your running or stop running for seven to ten days. When the pain has subsided, do some stretching and strengthening exercises. Two good ones for stretching are Foot on Table, Knee Forward and the Butterfly. For strengthening the adductors, do the Inner Thigh Lift. You'll find all these in the Exercise chapter.

After seven days of doing these exercises and not running, you can start running gently. Just a mile or so a day. Keep up the exercises and increase your mileage gradually.

If the pain persists, take a few days off from running. Continue your exercises. Then try running again. You may cure your problem with this treatment. Or you may have to go to a podiatrist for orthotics. He may decide you need the inner heel wedge I described earlier.

Curing groin pull takes a lot of persistence on your part and a real devotion to your exercises. One runner who did beat this problem is my friend and patient, Nancy Tighe.

Nancy is a tall, slim forty-eight-year-old who helps run her husband's ad agency for a living and then goes out and runs marathons for fun. Except, it got to be less and less fun because she kept getting pain in the adductor muscles.

The first time Nancy got a clue as to the cause of her problem was when she attended a lecture by Dr. Schuster. He said that groin pulls can happen when we run on slippery pavement and Nancy had just completed a thirty kilometer race in the snow (over eighteen miles).

But Nancy's problem did not come only from slippery streets. The groin pull kept recurring as she upped her mileage

in training for marathons. She would have to cut her mileage—
sometimes to nothing. Twice she had to skip marathons she
had been training for. Once she completed a marathon, but
had to jog the whole thing. It took her four hours and thirteen
minutes to finish.

Nancy kept talking to people, trying to find an answer to
her problem. Some of the suggestions were disastrous and actually made the pain worse. Finally she wound up in my office,
and I ordered orthotics for her with the inner-heel wedge described earlier. These seemed to do the trick—along with
stretching and strengthening exercises. She does the Inner
Thigh Lift with one pound weights on her ankles. I spoke to
Nancy this afternoon, and she told me she's hard at work
training for a marathon—doing sixty miles a week, pain free.

Back Thigh/Back Knee Pains

(Hamstring pull or sciatica)

Seymour Goldstein, D.C.

To advise you on this subject, I've called on a man who's a
genius at hamstrings—Dr. Seymour (Mac) Goldstein, a
chiropractor who is doctor and advisor for the Olympic In-
vitational Meet and for many track teams, such as the Brooklyn Atoms. He's consultant to coaches at NYU, Fairleigh
Dickinson, Brown and many other East Coast colleges that
are involved in track. Here's Dr. Goldstein's advice for runners with pain in the back of the thigh.

If you feel pain in the back of the thigh, you may have pulled
your hamstring muscle. Or you may have sciatica.

It's important for you to find out which it is—because sciatica is a problem you really can't treat yourself. Take it to a
doctor—a GP, chiropractor, orthopedist or osteopath.

Here are a few ways to tell the difference between sciatica
and hamstring pull.

• Exactly where is the pain located? If the pain is centered down the back of the thigh, it's probably hamstring pull. If it's toward the outer side of the thigh, it's probably sciatica. With sciatica, you may also feel pain in the hip and lower back, and the pain may extend down to the foot.

· If you have hamstring pull, you'll find it very painful to extend your leg. Your knee wants to stay bent.

· Lie on your back. Raise one leg, knee straight. Have someone flex your foot—that is, bend your toe toward your knee. This will be very painful if you have sciatica. You'll feel a burning sensation or electric shock down the back of your leg or in the small of the back or in one buttock.

Repeat the test on the other leg.

If you have hamstring pull, you won't even be able to complete the test, because you won't be able to stretch your leg out straight.

· Feel the back of your thigh with your fingertips. Look for a lump. This is a contraction in the muscle. If you find this lump, you have hamstring pull. Sometimes you'll even see a black and blue mark that looks like a bruise—as if someone had punched you. That's because, in hamstring pull, the muscle fibers may tear. That's what causes the black and blue mark.

As I said, sciatica must be treated by your doctor. With hamstring pull—or a hamstring cramp—there are some things you can do to help yourself. The treatment for these two hamstring problems is the same, but the cramp will clear up in a few days, while the pull takes at least a few weeks.

The hamstring is a muscle extending from the back of the knee to the buttocks. It has contracted and become painful because you've overextended it or given it a number of quick extensions.

That's what you do when you're sprinting, and when you're running downhill. Sprinters often get hamstring pull because they're always stretching their legs to the limit. Joggers don't get it very often, because they keep their knees bent. A sprinter with hamstring problems has to become a Long Slow Distance runner until his muscles ease up.

Hamstring pull is more common in cold weather, because runners don't warm up their muscles enough.

It's also a pre-marathon injury. Say you've been running gently for months, building up your distance at a fairly comfortable pace. Now the time for the marathon comes close and you decide you want to break three hours—or whatever your goal is. So you start doing intervals, pushing for speed—and extending your legs more than usual. That's when you may get hamstring pull.

You may complete a marathon with hamstring pull, but you won't set a new personal record. You have to use a short stride and a high knee lift, because it's painful to extend the leg. You may even have trouble walking—but you can still jog.

So sprinting is one way you may overextend your legs. Another way is running on a banked track. When you do this, you're giving yourself one "short leg." For instance, say your right leg is on the upper side of the slope. It becomes the short leg—so it has to overextend itself, to keep up with the "long" leg. The solution is to reverse directions.

Or, you may really have one short leg. That's another cause for overextending. Be sure to read the section in this book that tells you how to check your leg lengths, and how to treat yourself for Short Leg. In that section, Dr. Weisenfeld tells you to check to see whether your hipbones are level—because "short leg" is often caused by hipbones that are not level. This is called pelvic tilt. Correcting pelvic tilt is one way that chiropractors and osteopaths correct hamstring pull.

There are some things you can do to treat hamstring pull yourself. How long should you try home treatment before seeing a doctor? I'd say if you just have a cramp in the muscle, it will ease up in about three days. If you have hamstring pull, work with it for a week to ten days. In that time you should have enough relief so you know you're doing the right thing. If you don't have much relief within ten days, see a chiropractor or osteopath. Because the longer your problem continues, the longer it will take to relieve it.

Now, here's your treatment.

• Keep running—or I should say, jogging. Take short steps so you don't have to extend your legs.

• If you've been running on a banked track and have hamstring pull in one leg only—reverse directions.

• Do exercises to stretch and strengthen the muscles. The two I recommend are Weighted Leg Extensions and Bent-Leg Sit-ups. They're both in the Exercise chapter of this book.

• Use ice before and after running. Put an ice pack on the sore muscle for a half hour before running, and a half hour after. This is one point on which Dr. Weisenfeld and I disagree. He never advises runners to use ice before running. Of course, we've all heard that you should never run with "cold" muscles. I'll tell you why I make an exception in this case.

When you have hamstring pull, your muscle is tight and inflamed—it hurts to extend it. But extending is just what it needs. So the ice anesthetizes the pain and brings down the inflammation. Now you're able to get out and jog—extend the leg to some degree—and this is part of your cure.

So, to sum up—your treatment for hamstring pull is:

• Treat yourself for short leg if necessary.

• If you've been running on a banked track, reverse direction.

• Don't stop running. Jog with short steps.

• Exercise

• Ice

If you haven't made much progress in about ten days, I'd advise you to see a chiropractor. He may use electrical stimulation to relax the muscle. And, if you have a short leg caused by pelvic tilt, he'll certainly work on straightening that out— so you can get rid of the basic cause of your hamstring pull.

Varicose Veins

If you've got varicose veins, you've chosen the right sport. Running can't reverse the varicosities you've got now, but it will probably help prevent or diminish further varicosities.

You see, the heart sends fresh, oxygen-filled blood to various parts of the body. But once the blood has been stripped of its oxygen and nutrients, the heart needs help in pumping the used blood back up again for refilling and reconditioning. The veins themselves, with the help of the muscles, perform a milking action that presses the blood back up.

What keeps that used blood from trickling back down again? You've got a series of valves in your veins. These valves let the blood through as it flows upward, but don't let it flow down again.

People with varicose veins have inherited a tendency to weak valves. The used blood is allowed to flow back down and pool in the legs.

By running, you're supplying extra muscular contractions to push the blood back up in the right direction. Running develops the musculature and supportive tissue in the legs. So keep on with your running.

Incidentally, when you've finished a run, it's very important not to make a sudden stop. While you're running, you're pumping blood hard. Now when you cross the finish line, if you stop suddenly, the pumping stops suddenly and the blood can pool in your legs. So keep on walking till your heart slows down and you stop huffing and puffing. This is important for everyone, not just for people with varicose veins.

Other ways you can help yourself: Don't sit for too long at a time. You're sitting on the veins and keeping the blood from moving. Get up and walk around during the day. Also, don't stand in one place for a long time. When you're standing in one place, your blood stands in one place and gravity pulls it down. Your whole aim is to keep it moving.

People with varicose veins have a tendency toward clotting —thrombophlebitis—if they're very inactive. That's why, in hospitals, people who've had surgery for varicose veins are kept moving. The nurse tries to get the patient out of bed right after surgery. They put elasticized stockings on the patient and elevate the legs to keep the blood moving.

Don't wear pants that tie tightly around the ankle. In the

old days, women were warned against wearing elastic garters around their thighs—but I don't think this is a problem now. Panty girdles that compress the thighs are harmful too.

Any pressure on the veins makes it hard for them to pump the blood up. That's why women with an inherited tendency toward this problem develop varicose veins during pregnancy. The weight of the uterus is putting extra pressure on the veins.

For veins that are severely distended, women can get some relief by wearing support pantyhose while running. If the pantyhose have elasticized feet, cut the lower part of the feet off because your feet swell when you run.

Men can wear support socks while running. I have varicose veins, and I never buy anything but support hose. It's worth paying a few cents more to get that extra relief.

If varicose veins become very painful, your best solution is injection therapy or surgery by a physician trained in the treatment of varicose veins.

Hip and Back Pains

Stanley Roman, D.O.

Dr. Roman is an osteopath who treats a lot of runners with hip and back problems. Sometimes patients come to me with these problems and I can help them with podiatry, but often, they also need a specialist for their particular injury. I send them to Dr. Roman because he is well-known for his success in getting those aching backs comfortable again and getting those nervous runners back on the road.

• Your feet may be giving you a pain in the back.
• That ache in your hip could be coming from your legs.
• A nerve in your spine may be causing a pain in your foot.

Back pain can be a tough mystery to solve. And I gave you those little clues to suggest something to you: If you have a hip or back pain, you have to look at the whole picture. No one can say ah ha! For that pain in the left hip, you should do such and such an exercise.

Your spinal column, hips, legs and feet all affect each other. So it's especially important for you, a runner, to know what's going on with your pelvis and spine.

Runners know a lot about their feet and legs. But their interest seems to stop there. They don't pay nearly as much attention to what happens north of the quadriceps until they get some back pain.

When you're running, every shock and jolt that happens to your feet is transferred right up to the hips and spine. If you're reading this chapter, I'll assume you've got some kind of pain in the back or hips. But, before we discuss your individual symptoms, you'll have to look at your overall body, and I'll outline a fifteen-minute checkup you should take. It will give you a pretty good first acquaintance with your skeleton. After that introduction, we'll discuss your individual symptoms and you'll be better able to understand them. The problems we'll discuss are the ones I see most in runners:

- Sciatica (Some symptoms of sciatica are pain in the lower buttock; pain down one leg; pain in lower back, on one side.)
- Low back pain.
- Side-of-hip pain.

But before you start your examination, let me give you some reassurance about your back problem. I'm sure you had a grandfather or a great aunt who always had to be "careful not to throw my back out." They treated themselves like invalids, thereby turning themselves into invalids.

These days, we're learning better. We've learned that, if you've got a back problem, there's probably nothing wrong with the way your back is made. But there probably *is* something wrong with the way you treat your back. Specifically, you've allowed your back muscles to get weak or tense through lack of exercise.

So your back problem can very likely be cured.

These days, we don't tell people with back problems to *avoid* exercise. We tell them to follow a carefully graded program of exercise. We'll give you some exercises here to handle the problems I see most often in runners. But if you have a chronic back problem that these exercises don't relieve, I suggest you get Dr. Han S. Kraus's book, *The Cause, Prevention, and Treatment of Backache.*

Another reassurance—this time about arthritis. Patients sometimes ask me whether the pounding action of running would trigger arthritis or make it worse. A Finnish study indicated that long distance runners have a lower incidence of arthritis—in fact, half as much—as compared to non-runners. Of course, the Finns don't run on paved roads as much as we do. So if you are worried about arthritis, try running on dirt roads. But by all means keep running—and keep up your supplementary exercise. They are especially important for the runner with arthritis.

You have to exercise the affected area to keep the joints mobile. If arthritis affects your back, be absolutely faithful about doing your back exercises. If it's your knees or hips that get arthritis, keep them well-exercised. Swimming is a good exercise to keep your whole body moving smoothly. Anyone with arthritis should keep his doctor informed on his condition, and he should keep active.

All right, enough discussion. Now you're ready to start your examination. I've included a checklist for you to fill in as you do your checkup. You'll be checking the straightness of your spine and shoulders; whether your pelvis is level or tilted. Whether your legs match in length. You'll find out if your abdominal muscles and lower back muscles are strong enough. You'll take a test for sciatic pain. And you'll check your feet, for balance.

Make notes on the checklist as you go along.

It may seem like a lot of trouble to give yourself this examination, but it's the only way to get at the cause of your back problem.

First, check your overall symmetry. You'll need a mirror or mirrors that give you a front-and-back view. You should not have to twist around to see your back, because then you won't be standing straight.

Okay, set up your mirrors and then stand in front of them, naked.

Checklist

1. Spine—any curves above or below waist? _____

2. Shoulders level? _____

3. Swayback—can you get back almost flat against wall, without bending knees? _____

4. Pelvis level, front view? _____

5. Pelvis level, back view? _____

6. Leg length equal, lying down? _____

7. Sciatica test: pain in either leg? _____

8. Sit-up: strain in abdominal muscles? _____

9. Lower back test: can you hold leg lift for ten seconds? _____

10. Feet: Fallen arches? _____ Long first toe? _____

---

1. *Spine.* Your spine should run straight down your back. There should be no curves toward the left or right sides. Look for the bumps of the vertebrae, and follow that line down to see if it's straight. Look for curves above the waist or below the waist. They could be a reason for back pains, hip pains, leg pains.

Look at your shoulder blades—see if they're level.

2. *Shoulders.* Stand straight in front of the mirror, and see whether your shoulders are level.

3. *Check for swayback.* Stand with your back against the

wall and try to get your back as flat as possible without bending your knees. Your waist should be close to the wall in back. You should not be able to slip a flat hand between the wall and your back.

4. *Pelvis, front view*   Take a felt-tipped pen and put a dot on each hip bone. Now hold a string between the two dots and see if the string is level.

5. *Pelvis, back view.*   You'll need a helper for this. He or she should put a dot in the dimple above each buttock. He should put the dot close to the spine, not toward the side of the body. Now he should draw a line across the top of each hipbone. To do this, he feels for the outline of the bone, and draws the line there. Now he looks at the dots. Are the hipbones level or is one higher than the other? Are the dots in the dimples level?

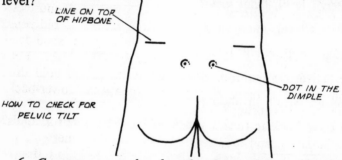

LINE ON TOP
OF HIPBONE

DOT IN THE
DIMPLE

HOW TO CHECK FOR
PELVIC TILT

6. *Compare your leg lengths, lying down.*   Again, you need someone to help you. Lie on your back. Your helper makes sure you're lying flat, with your pelvis even—you're not hitching one leg up. Now he holds both ankles and pulls on them to straighten your legs. Then he compares the ankle bones on the inner side of the leg. If the two ankle bones are not on the same level, then one leg is short.

7. *Sciatica.*   While you're lying on your back, do the test for sciatica. Lift your right leg up, with the knee straight. Now your helper holds your foot and bends the toe toward the knee. If this causes a pain in the leg, you have sciatica. Anyone will feel some degree of tightness and resistance to this foot-flexing. But if it's a definite pain, you should suspect

sciatica. Lower your leg and repeat the test with the other leg. Sciatica is not something you can treat yourself. Go to your family GP or an osteopath or an orthopedist.

8. *Abdominal muscles.* Test your abdominal muscles by doing a bent-leg sit-up. Lie on your back, with your feet on the floor and your knees bent. Your feet should be as close to your body as possible. Put your hands behind your head. Your helper holds your feet down. Try to sit up to a full sitting position. If you feel strain in the abdominal muscles (not just effort, but real strain), then you have weak abdominal muscles. They could be a cause of your back problem. If this exercise is hard for you to do, don't force it. You'll have to work gradually on your abdominal exercises until you're ready to do the complete sit-up.

9. *Lower back muscles.* Test your lower back muscles. Lie on your stomach with a pillow under your hips. Fold your arms under your head. Your helper holds your shoulders down as you lift your legs. Keep your knees straight. You should be able to get your thighs off the floor and hold this position for ten seconds. If you can't, then weak lower-back muscles may be causing your back pain.

10. *Fallen arches—weak foot.* Check your feet for fallen arches. Stand up and look at the arches on the inner side of the foot. See if your arch flattens out—so it almost disappears. This is called "pronating"—the weight shifting to the inner side of the foot. This weight shift could be a cause of back pain.

Now, notice your toe lengths. If the second toe is longer than the big toe, this could cause a weight imbalance. This condition is called Morton's foot.

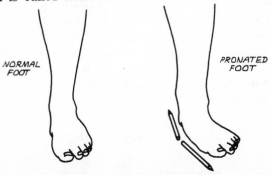

NORMAL FOOT   PRONATED FOOT

If you have either of these problems, you should take care of them because they're likely to cause you some aches and pains—in the back or elsewhere.

For Morton's foot, you should probably go to your podiatrist and let him check out your whole foot for imbalances. If you have fallen arches (weak foot), you'll probably end up going to the podiatrist, too. But there's a section in this book on weak foot which will give you some ways you can help the problem by yourself.

Now we've completed the examination that everyone should take for back pain. So we're ready to discuss your individual problems. The three most common back problems I see in runners are sciatica, low back pain and side of hip pain.

Sciatica   Symptoms could be pain in the lower buttock, on one side; or pain down one leg, sometimes all the way to the foot; pain in lower back on one side.

As I said, sciatica is not something you can treat yourself.

The sciatic nerve is the longest nerve in your body. It's formed by nerve roots at the end of the spine. From there it passes through the pelvis and into the legs. Its branches go all the way to the foot. If you feel pain anywhere along the sciatic nerve, there could be a pinching somewhere along the nerve. This could be caused by a pelvic tilt or by pressure on a disc.

A disc is a small package of jellylike material that separates one vertebra from another and gives the spine some cushioning. For various reasons, some of the disc may protrude out— so it's not all centered between its two vertebrae. This might happen because a pulled muscle is causing pressure. A tight, spasmodic muscle could do it.

Runners sometimes feel a pain down the back of the thigh and assume that it's a muscle pull—when actually, it's sciatica.

You can tell the difference by doing the test for sciatica that I gave you earlier. If you feel a sharp pain when your foot is flexed, you should assume it's sciatica, and go see your doctor. (If you don't feel that pain, you may have pulled a hamstring muscle—and you should read the section in this book on hamstring pull.)

Sciatica is something that may linger for months. And that means you can't run for months. Or it may just flare up and disappear again. There's an old belief that once you've had sciatica, it will probably come back. Actually, there may be years between incidents. You may always have the tendency, but you should not be nervously expecting the next attack. Just follow your doctor's instructions and assume that you'll be out running again soon.

Make an appointment with your family doctor or an osteopath or an orthopedist and meanwhile, stop running. Take hot baths or go to the steam room. Take aspirin to reduce the inflammation. Don't do leg-stretching exercises, because that could make the inflammation worse.

Low Back Pain   This is the most frequent back problem I see in runners.

If you have low back pain, or pain in one hip, you may have found one or two things in your examination: uneven pelvis (it's called pelvic tilt) or unequal leg lengths.

It's easy to understand why either of these would cause pain. If your pelvis is tilted, it means the muscles on one side are pulled; they're under tension. This is enough to cause pain. Now add the jarring motion of running—and the muscles may go into spasm.

The first aid treatment for low back pain has 3 steps:

1. Rest—cut down your running.
2. Two aspirins with each meal to reduce inflammation and pain.
3. Moist heat. Take hot baths or go to the steam room. I find these more effective than heating pads or heat rubs.

The long-term treatment has two steps: First, treat yourself for short-leg. Second, strengthen the muscles in your lower back and abdomen.

First, treat yourself for short-leg.   Why should you treat yourself for short-leg? Because pelvic tilt and short-leg go together. It works like this: If you have one short leg, your pelvis may tilt to compensate for it. Conversely, if you have a pelvic tilt, your pelvis is pulling one leg up. So that leg *is* shorter, in effect.

The reason I had you compare your legs lying down was to see if you really have a short leg—or if it's just the pelvis that's pulling it up, so it seems shorter when you're standing.

In any case, treat yourself for short-leg by putting a heel pad in one shoe. Start with a pad ³⁄₁₆-inch thick—even if your leg is ½-inch or 1-inch short. Don't try to correct for the full inch.

To make your heel lift, get surgical felt and layer it until it's ³⁄₁₆-inch thick. Or, some shoemakers have hard rubber heel lifts you can wear inside your shoe.

I never use sponge rubber for heel lifts because they compress down when you stand on them. I know that Dr. Weisenfeld does recommend sponge rubber lifts because he feels the cushioning gives you good shock absorption. Since the sponge rubber does press down, Dr. Weisenfeld will tell you to use almost a ½-inch of sponge rubber for ½-inch difference in leg lengths. But in my practice, I use the less compressible material.

Use your heel lift and do your exercises, and you should get relief in about a week. If you get NO relief, the heel lift may not be helping you, so you should remove it. My feeling is, if a heel lift isn't doing you any good, it's better not to wear one. Your body may be used to functioning with two different leg lengths. And if it's working okay, let's not disturb it.

For the same reason, a person with a short-leg but no pain should not use a heel lift.

Second, strengthen your back and abdominal muscles. You'll have to do exercises to strengthen the abdomen and the lower back. You've probably heard that the abdominal muscles support the lower back, and this is true. But if you have lower-back pain, it's safe to say you should strengthen your lower back muscles too.

Bent-Leg Situps strengthen your abdominal muscles. Hip

Rolls strengthen the lower back. Knee Lifts strengthen the lower back and the abdominal muscles. You'll find all these in the Exercise chapter.

Side-of-Hip Pains   Some people feel this pain at the joint of the hip and thigh. Some people feel it up a bit higher—toward the hip bone.

Side-of-hip pain is an overuse injury. It's an inflammation of the fascia, a fibrous, somewhat flexible material that's found in the hips, legs and many other places in the body. The inflammation may start with the tendons that attach the muscles to the bones; then the inflammation spreads to the fascia.

If there's something wrong with your lower back—like weak back muscles—the problem can be passed along to the fascia at the side of the hip.

If you're using your legs incorrectly when you run, that error can be passed along to the side-of-hip fascia.

You can probably get rid of this pain—but it takes some persistence on your part. The fact is, some exercises and techniques help some people and others help other people. I'll give you some techniques that both Dr. Weisenfeld and I use on our patients. These remedies do work—but I can't tell you which will work for you.

1. If you like swimming, swim on your back and do the frog kick.

2. In running, shorten your stride.

3. If you're running on a hard surface, switch to a soft surface. If you're running on a soft surface, switch to a hard surface.

4. Change the kind of shoes you're wearing. Don't just get another pair of the same style—get a different style. Get one with a higher heel or a lower heel. Get one that's broader at the ball of the foot, or narrower. Get a shoe with a higher counter, or a lower one.

5. Do Hip Rolls and Knee Lifts to strengthen your lower back. These are described in the Exercise chapter.

Index